"Wander, look for lands . . . send pioneers ahead, have them plant maize, when the harvest is ready, move up to it—keep me, Huitzilopochtli, always with you, carrying me like a banner, feed me on human hearts torn from the recently sacrificed . . ."

The Aztec did as their god commanded. They conquered and sacrificed, planted and reaped. And in so doing they created a form of life whose luxury has never been equalled by any of the other peoples of America.

Victor W. von Hagen, scientist and writer, explores the fabulous Aztec world in this richly illustrated book. He covers the whole of their complex civilization—from the political and social structure of their democratic city-state to their method of preparing human beings for religious sacrifice. He tells how the Aztec made war and conquest the basic pattern of their daily life. He analyzes their advanced forms of art, writing and sculpture. And he describes their temples and palaces, particularly the splendor of Moctezuma's kingdom, the lavish city of Tenochtitlán, built in the midst of a salt lake, deep in the interior of Mexico.

This fascinating history of the Aztec, a tribe of people who forever left their impress on the continent of America, is illustrated with 16 pages of photographs. It also features over 50 drawings by Alberto Beltran, winner of the Pan-American Prize (the first prize for drawing) in the First Biennial of Painting and Drawing sponsored by the Universidad Nacional of Mexico.

Other Books by VICTOR W. von HAGEN

EXPLORATION:

Off With Their Heads (1937)
Ecuador the Unknown (1938)
Jungle in the Clouds (1940)
Ecuador and the Galapagos Islands: A History (1949)
Highway of the Sun (1955)

BIOGRAPHY:

South America Called Them (1945)
Maya Explorer, The Life of John Lloyd Stephens (1947)
Frederick Catherwood, Architect (1950)
The Four Seasons of Manuela (1952)

ETHNOLOGY:

The Tsatchela Indians of Western Ecuador (1939)
The Jicaque Indians of Honduras (1940)
The Maya and Aztec Papermakers (1943)
Realm of the Incas (1957)

Victor W. von Hagen

THE AZTEC:
MAN AND TRIBE

Illustrated by ALBERTO BELTRAN

Mentor: Ancient Civilizations
Published by THE NEW AMERICAN LIBRARY

ACKNOWLEDGMENTS

The author wishes to thank the following publishers for their kind permission to reprint from the books indicated below.

Farrar, Straus and Cudahy, Inc.: *The Discovery and Conquest of Mexico, 1517-1521*, by Bernal Díaz del Castillo, translated by A. P. Maudslay. Copyright 1956 by Farrar, Straus and Cudahy. Used by permission of the publishers, Farrar, Straus and Cudahy, Inc.

Routledge & Kegan Paul Ltd.: *The Discovery and Conquest of Mexico, 1517-1521*, by Bernal Díaz del Castillo, translated by A. P. Maudslay.

Five Letters, 1519-1526, by Hernando Cortés, translated by J. Bayard Morris.

LIBRARY OF CONGRESS CATALOG CARD NO. 58-12837

*MENTOR BOOKS are published by
The New American Library of World Literature, Inc.
501 Madison Avenue, New York 22, New York*

PRINTED IN THE UNITED STATES OF AMERICA

For my grandson
Philippe Evariste Victor Bordaz
future archaeologist

"Is there such a thing as an impartial history? And what is history? The written representation of past events. But what is an event . . . ? It is a notable fact. Now, how is the historian to discriminate whether a fact is notable or no? He decides this arbitrarily, according to his character and idiosyncrasy, at his own taste and fancy—in a word, as an artist. . . ."

The Gardens of Epicurus.

CONTENTS

FIGURES

PLATES

(Plates 1-21 will be found as a complete section between pp. 112 and 113.)

I

THE HISTORICAL
AND GEOGRAPHICAL BACKGROUND
OF THE AZTEC

1. Of Archaeological Explorers—and Time

The Aztec, of course, were not called Aztec. And very definitely they were not an empire. Moreover they arrived so late on the Mexican scene and were so unimportant when they did come to the lakes, which was Mexico, that not a single tribe recorded their arrival. Their "kings" were in reality elected "speakers" and there were no "halls of Montezuma" (except in song), so that the misconception of there being an "Aztec Empire" is actually a non sequitur of history just as was in fact the Holy Roman Empire (which was neither holy, Roman, nor an empire).

Still the Tenochas called "Aztec" were the first of the ancient Sun Kingdoms to be made known to the other world and the first to tumble into Europe's lap, and with this dramatic impact on man's imagination the first impressions cannot be undone; we remain stuck with the "Aztec Empire."

How and why this barbaric American Sun Kingdom fell into the hands of a relatively few *conquistadores* is a twice-told tale; still, no matter how often retold, it never loses its wonderment—how "stout Cortés" made his way into the heartland of Tenochtitlán, seized its "king" and forced it to accept a *pax hispaniensis*.[1]

The literature on the Aztec is simply overwhelming. There seems not a phase of their life that has not been explored, analyzed and written up; their origins, history, and rebus-writing, their religion and calendar, have been gone over again and again; that which remains of their glyph-scripts has been published; excavations within and outside the traditional

Fig. 1. Archaeological sites which form part of this history.

"Aztec Empire" territory are being carried out progressively; for more than two decades reports, well-documented and learned, continue to be issued at a rate that is truly astounding. For almost two hundred years some of the great names in literature have written on the Aztec and their neighbors— and when all of this is seen together in one library it is so formidable in quantity and quality that it would seem almost an impertinence for anyone to write another book on the Aztec. And yet. . . .

And yet since the Aztec arrived so very late on the Mexican scene (there were so many cultures before them), and since they were magic-bound every moment of their lives—peopling their world with gods and symbols—there has remained much bewilderment in the literature. More: since the history of the Aztec (which involves mythology, astronomy, ethnology, and search into all that went on thousands of years before them) is complicated, it is not always an easy subject to write on or to read about.

There is very little in this life that is definitive, and there is seldom a book that exhausts a subject, particularly one so involved as the Aztec. The old Roman who said on his death-bed that "much remains to be done and much will still remain nor shall any man after the revolution of a thousand ages be denied the opportunity of contributing something" could well have been speaking of the Aztec. A concise new book on them does not have to beg its own apology.

There now is no lack of literary ammunition for it. It was the plaint of William Prescott when he began to write his celebrated *History of the Conquest of Mexico* in 1839,[2] that he had to cast his cannons before he fired them, meaning that he had to create his own holograph library by having all the unpublished manuscripts copied in Spain before he could begin. Such is far from the situation now—the material at one's disposal is awesome.

The Spanish conquerors of the Aztec were for the most part lettered and literate and they felt historicity of the moment. Hernán Cortés, who reported history as he made it, was, for his time, considered to be a man of learning; he had attended the University of Salamanca. His famous *Five Letters*[3] to his King-Emperor, written between the intervals of battle, are as alive as if printed in blood. There were others, too, who wrote of the conquest while the flesh of history was still warm. An "Anonymous Conqueror"[4] wrote a *Narrative of Some Things of New Spain and the Great City of Temestitan;* another, one Andres de Tapia, who involved himself as much with women as conquest, left his literary impressions of the fall of the Aztec, a book which pushed him up as it pulled his captain, Cortés, down.[5] The most literary of the chroniclers, Francisco de Gómara, penned his *Chronicle of the Conquest of New Spain*,[6] and as he was the household chaplain to Cortés, then Marquis of the Valley and full of riches and renown, he blew the glorification of Cortés theme so onesided that it set an old war horse of the conquest, Bernal Díaz del Castillo ("I am now an old man over eighty-four years of age and I have lost my sight and hearing . . ."), to dictate his wonderful and ageless *The Discovery and Conquest of Mexico*.[7]

The crusading padres continued the literature where the soldiers left off. In their efforts to effect the change within Mexico from one mythology to another, they perforce studied the languages, the myths, and the round of daily life of the peoples. The most indefatigable of these was Bernardino de Sahagun,[8] who arrived in Mexico in 1529 and who left, after decades of devoted study, a history of the life and times of a people that is invaluable to any who work on the Aztec. And there were many others.[9] The literature is deepened because of them as well as by such as Dr. Francisco Hernández, a physician sent out by the King of Spain to examine the new plants of the "newfounde worlde"; his five-year plant exploration with the aid of numerous native scribes and artists is one of the great monuments of botanical science [10] and from it we have a wonderful glimpse into Aztec earth-knowledge.

The seventeenth century belonged to the padres; it was the period of printed vocabularies, dictionaries of Indian languages, breviaries, and a sort of demi-history—a literature they termed "relaciones." But the eighteenth century brought the Enlightenment and with it an interest in the past, the sort of romantic speculation that appears in Count Volney's rhapsodic elegy to *Les Ruines*.[11] Interest in "ruins of empires" appeared with nature worship and was a "product of good communications," for in the seventeenth century all sensible men disliked wild nature but when European road systems began to be overhauled and one could journey in comparative comfort, interest began again in nature—and ruins. This fashion spilled over into Mexico, where first in 1773 the Maya ruins of Palenque were discovered,[12] then the awesome temple of the Plumed Serpent at Xochicalco was brought to public attention.[13] This fever for the "antique" reached its crescendo when, in the course of altering the foundations of the cathedral in Mexico in 1790, workmen came across the gigantic Aztec calendar stone, buried since 1521. Scholars in

Europe were then seeking to unravel the Egyptian hieroglyphics; the learned world made much over symbols; the
romantic agony was at hand and intellectual interest was rekindled in the remains of the "Aztec Empire."

The youthful Alexander von Humboldt arrived in Mexico
in 1803 after four years of strenuous exploration in South
America,[14] and with him and *Les Ruines,* the whole of the
then available Mexican antique was recast in a modern scientific mold. He brought together all the known drawings of
ruins; the Aztec codices that he did not find in Mexico he
sought out in Rome, Berlin and Dresden; these, and the first
good reproductions of "American" art as well, he published
in 1810 in one handsome folio.[15]

After Humboldt there were enough gods, graves, and
scholars to fill a new *Iliad.* The fabulous Count Waldeck of
dubious genealogy appeared early in the nineteenth century
in Mexico as a designer of drop-curtains for the theater.
When he matured into archaeology, made his way into Yucatan, and limned some of the Maya structures, they were
beautifully inaccurate, with his purposeful falsifications of
elephant trunks and Phoenicians, and helped to create the
"lunatic fringe" in American archaeology. The only positive
fact about Waldeck is the date of his death.[16] John Lloyd
Stephens, the New York lawyer turned archaeological explorer, was at almost the same time exploring the whole of
Mayadom. Because of his accurate descriptions and fine
critical sense—nor can one overlook the superb illustrations of
Frederick Catherwood—the whole field of Mexican archaeology felt and continues to feel the impulse of these splendid
books.[17]

At the same time in England, Edward King, Viscount
Kingsborough, who had never seen an American Indian in
his life—nor wanted to (for he had already preconceived
Indians as origined out of the wandering tribes of Israel)—was
publishing *nine* folio volumes of reproductions of all the known
glyph writings of the Maya and Aztec to prove his "American
Indians are Jews" theory. It cost him his fortune and his life.[18]
But by 1843 William Prescott had given the Indians back to
the Indians by the publication of his *History of the Conquest
of Mexico.* The effect of the *Conquest* was felt strongly in all
of the world's literary circles. It shamed Spanish historians
(who had neglected the theme) that a half-blind American
lawyer who had never seen Mexico should have published
what they themselves ought to have written. The resultant
effect: the manuscripts lying moldering in the Spanish archives
for centuries were published.

Since then no one nation has had a Mexican monopoly. The North Americans, beginning with Stephens and Prescott, have continued on uninterruptedly for a century; the late George Vaillant, Samuel Lothrop, Matthew Stirling and Gordon Ekholm, to mention only a few, represent the tradition. The British have never been far behind; they have maintained the line from Catherwood to Maudslay, from Zelia Nuttall to T. A. Joyce.[19] It continues with C. A. Burland of the British Museum who carries on the inheritance. The Swedes have also been interested in Mexico long before the comparative studies of Baron Nordenskiöld were published; now Sigvald Linné works on it.

The Germans have been active in the Mexican field ever since Humboldt wrote his first book and brought back to Berlin its first glimpse of Mexican glyph writing; from Eduard Seler to Förstmann (who helped decipher the Maya glyphs) to Hermann Beyer (who gave much substance to the theoretical studies), the interest and quality of scholarship have been continuous; Paul Kirchhoff [20] maintains it at the present day. The French have been interested since back in 1529, when André Thévet, cosmographer to the King of France, studied the Mexican Tribute Charts which a pirate had pocketed as his part of the rape of the Spanish convoy off Vera Cruz. From the 1840s, when the gentle aristocratic scholar Comte Adolphe de Circourt gave William Prescott aid, until the present-day scholarly work of Jacques Soustelle [21] (mentioned often in this book), the French have been stimulated by *le Mexicain*.

These last archaeological years have belonged to the Mexican scholars. Under them new ruins have been found, restored and investigated; careful stratigraphical work with advanced techniques has been carried out. The names of the Mexicans who have shown this wonderful capacity to examine their past are so many that a mere recitation of them all would sound like a bibliography—Manuel Gamio, Alfonso Caso, José García Payón, Eduardo Noguera, Ignacio Marquina,[22] to mention only a few—and books, pamphlets, papers, continue to flow daily out of all this archaeological activity. The result is that the date of emergence of early Man in Mexico is continually being pushed back.

All this activity has given rise to a general interest in everything that has formed Man's past (for the past is contained in the present just as the properties of a triangle are involved in its definition) and there has been much public interest in the literature. Unfortunately, to have a generous panorama requires lengthy and involved reading. And so while the general reader would like to know something of all this, still the sheer bulk of the material. . . .

In this book I, as author, have leaned heavily on much of this literature of the five centuries. I have attempted ("according to my character and idiosyncrasy," to paraphrase the *Gardens of Epicurus,* "of my own taste and fancy—in a word, as an artist") to select what I regarded as pertinent. Of the twenty years I have given to ethno-geographical exploration of the tropical Americas, more than five have been spent in Middle America and Mexico. At a sufficiently early date (1931) I set off to find the origins of Aztec and Maya papermaking, then to study the biology and geographical distribution of the quetzal, royal bird of the Aztec, and, in the process, to capture one too, for the first time in history; later to write the biographies of those archaeological explorers of the Americas who represented the *Zeitgeist* of their time.[23] So that all of these varied activities have given me some idea of "local conditions"; thus my selections and prejudices as to what is pertinent to the Aztec are, in a measure, qualified. I have tried to determine, in my manner, the essential quality of the Aztec and put it down in such a literary form as to attract, and not to frighten off before it instructs, the general and curious reader. And at all times aiming at simplicity, with the object of following the advice of Anatole France, who said to a young writer: "I begin to ask myself whether supreme talent may not consist of writing very simply about very complicated matters."

2. The Setting

All Mexico is divided into two parts: the mountainous and the flat.

The land is one of extremes: the contrasts of the volcanic wastes, the high mesetas of thin air, the aridity of deserts, the lush parts folding one upon another, exiling valley from valley, has made this land the love and despair of man ever since he took possession of this Mexican earth.

If a figure must be devised for it, Mexico is shaped like a cornucopia, from the broad open tablelands of its northern boundaries, where bison once roamed, down a thousand miles south to the narrow isthmus where the land tumbles into mountains and tropical verdure with all the luxuriant richness

Fig. 2. The shape of Mexico; a schematic drawing that illustrates the physical isolation of cultures. The inset in black shows Aztec domination over Central Mexico by 1519.

that is centered there, where the Indians found jade, coral, shells, chocolate, amber, rubber, quetzal plumes—the paradise lands to the mountain-bound dweller.

Mexico has extremes in climate, and, even though half the land lies in the tropical zone, altitude is more important than latitude. The eastern coast is broader and fiercely rained on by the trades; it is more lush, and it was the ground for early civilizations—the land of the Olmec, Totonac, Huastec. The western coast has a narrower fringe of coastline: nature here is not so prodigal and this is reflected in the early cultures; they are threadbare compared to those on the "other side."

The Mexican land rises up from these two shores, sometimes abruptly, sometimes gradually, to the high plateau which is the bulk of the geography of Mexico. Orizaba, a snow-topped mountain (the Aztec called it Citlal-tepetl: "Mountain-of-the Star"), rises out of the verdured jungle to dominate at 18,000 feet the "cold-lands." Here there is a naked misery of soil as the first Spaniards found: ". . . three days' march through a desert land uninhabitable on account of its barrenness, lack of water and great cold. . . . Oh! the thirst and hunger suffered by the men assailed by whirlwind of hailstones and rain. . . ."

This high mesa-land, varying between 3,000 and 10,000 feet, is classic Mexican soil. It has a troubled geology. Volcanoes in times past and continuing up into the present have belched out stone and pumice, tufa and obsidian, transforming much of what could have been fertile valleys into desert wastes. Nature has given Mexico some of the most spectacular scenery in the world, but it has extracted a heavy toll from man who has lived there. There are few navigable rivers; much of the land mass is made sterile by the volcanic outpourings; there are long dry winters when dust storms carry off the loam and flash floods complete the ruin; there are high semi-desert areas which are covered with the thickets of chaparral—cactus, mesquite and sage. Then this direful aspect is replaced, in another region, with pine forests, and, when the land dips down into a watered zone, there are verdant exuberant valleys.

Mexico had no Nile-like valley. It had no oases such as appear along the two-thousand-mile-long Peruvian coast and provide an eternal loam even in a rainless land; it had no burden animals—not even the llama. The wheel, had they had it, would have done them no good at all since all is up and down, and high valley is walled from high valley almost throughout the length and breadth of the land; its heights are only passable to foot traffic.

Rain defines the seasons. On the high Mexican tableland it falls, the gods willing, between June and September; the rest of the months are dry except for a caprice of nature and then it will fall out of season and may even snow in Mexico City, an event often recorded by the Aztec in their glyph history of unusual events.

The gifts of sun and rain not being equal, much of the land has been inhospitable to man. So while Mexico is vast, much of it in ancient times was empty of man and the empty places were where the soil was naked and sterile. The really fertile areas had been occupied since the earliest times, especially that incunabula of culture, the valley of Anáhuac, the "land-on-the-edge-of-the-water," where Mexico City lies.

Where the mountains rise high in the center of the high Mexican plateau, where the cone of Popocatepetl rears snow-crowned, and beside it the reclining white-woman mountain, Ixtaccihuatl, there is a series of intermontane basins. These begin many miles northward around the fish-filled lakes of Michoacan and form a series of lagoons and lakes culminating about these snow-covered mountains in the valley of Anáhuac. Great civilizations sprang out of this soil; the Toltec, who left behind their immense "City of God" at Teotihuacán, and the related culture of Tula, farther to the north. The

Fig. 3. The distribution of pre-Aztec tribes and cultures throughout Central Mexico and Guatemala-Yucatan. The Aztec came into cultural being in the part occupied by the Toltec.

Fig. 4. The leaders of the Aztec, heads of four clans (with their symbols above their heads), make their way toward the valley of Mexico in A.D. 1168.

land height being less than 8,000 feet, corn, the essential, grows here, as does much of the other needed things; maguey is plentiful for fibers and the sweetish syrup from which the pulque intoxicant is prepared; the saline lakes yield salt, a primary basic need for cereal-eating peoples. The volcanoes erupting for untold centuries have piled up layer upon layer, forming inexhaustible rock quarries, source of the obsidian glass which when split became knives, weapons and razors, and when polished, mirrors; and, for sculpture, a hard gray volcanic stone, capable of being chipped; and a peculiar porous stuff, *tezontli,* used for building material.

Everything has its reasons—be they geographical or sociological. Imperialist cultures were born out of the harsh lands. In the tropic lands where man luxuriated in warmth and sensualism, the expansion mood was limited, but the man who came out of the high country, scoured by wind and hail, was the one with imperialistic ambitions—an effect of geography.

As the Inca in Peru, so the Aztec of Mexico; they came from the raw colder zones. By the time the Aztec emerged as tribe (circa A.D. 1200), the best lands were already occupied. They called themselves "Tenochas," descendants of northern tribes. In their search for land they had to run the gamut of numerous other peoples already settled who gave them disputed passage. The hard necessity of war breeds men; peoples grow by and against other peoples to inward greatness, and the Aztec were glebeless. They were, as others had been before them, far-ranging animals wandering from necessity—certainly in search of land or perhaps just out of the "primary microcosmic urgency to move." [24]

So into the lakes of Anáhuac in their year *Ome-Acatl,* 2-Cane (1168), moved this god-tormented tribe, this "Aztec" people who were to systematize rapine and war into a tribute-state and forever leave their impress on the Mexican land.

3. The Year of the Spaniard

What are the imponderables (called the genius of a people) that propel it forward and upward?

In 1168—a date fully accepted by historians—the Tenochas entered the lakes of Anáhuac from the northwest. Landless and friendless and already eyed with dismay by the other tribes settled about the lakes because of their readiness to offer human hearts to their gods, they had little of the outward trappings of human culture. A tribe small in numbers composed of contending clans and forced out of one settled region after another, they finally selected several islets two miles out in Lake Texcoco and, carrying their god's image before them, they began in 1325 to build their city-state.

Within two centuries they were the overlords of Mexico, and *Tenochtitlán,* the "Place-of-the-Tenochas," was the most sumptuous city ever raised by indigenous man in the Americas. The Spaniards who had arrived to make its conquest and add its land titles to those of their Emperor-King, Carlos V of Spain, entered "the great city of Tenochtitlán, Mexico, on the 8th of November . . . 1519."

"Gazing on such wonderful sights," wrote Bernal Díaz del Castillo [25] remembering it vividly after fifty years, "we did not know what to say or what appeared before us was real." They proceeded along a "causeway . . . eight paces in width" which ran "two miles from the mainland to the city . . . and so crowded with people there was hardly room for them all . . . the temples were full of people . . . and canoes came from all parts of the lake."

Being close to the entrance of the city, they were met by the "king's" entourage "and the great Moctezuma got down from his litter" and, supported by others, "continued beneath a marvellously rich canopy of green coloured feathers with much gold and silver embroidery and with pearls and jade suspended from a sort of bordering, which was wonderful to look at. The great Moctezuma was richly attired . . . many

Fig. 5. The valley of Anáhuac and the lakes of Mexico. Although they have five names, the lakes were actually a continuous body of water. Since there was no outlet, the water was mostly saline except in the southern parts (lakes Chalco and Xochimilco) which received fresh streams of water from the snow-topped volcanoes. The system of dikes and causeways was later developed by the Aztec so as to control the salinity of the lakes.

other lords walked before him sweeping the ground where he would tread and spreading cloths on it."

As they entered the city they were hardly able to believe their eyes. Bernal Díaz remembered that he "could not count the multitude of men and women and boys who were in the streets . . . in canoes on the canals who had come out to see us. It was indeed wonderful and, now that I am writing about it all"—he was then eighty-four—"it all comes before my eyes as though it had happened but yesterday."

Put to rest in "great halls and chambers canopied with the cloth of the country," they soon visited the *Uei Tlatoani*, the "First Speaker," Moctezuma, in his own immense quarters. Moctezuma lived in Lucullan luxury. "They prepared more than three hundred plates of the food that he was going to eat . . . but such a variety of dishes . . . so numerous that I cannot finish naming them. . . . Four very beautiful women brought water for his hands . . . other women brought him tortilla bread . . . he was served on Cholula earthenware. . . . From time to time they brought him, in cup-shaped vessels of pure gold, a certain drink made from chocolate. . . ."

Later Bernal Díaz del Castillo accompanied Cortés and "looked at the stored treasures of this Tribute-State and into where Moctezuma kept the accounts of all the revenue that was brought thither . . . in his books which were made of *amatl*-paper of which he had a great house full." And they saw the storehouses of cereals and maize, beans and peppers, brought in as tribute, other storehouses full of war dress, "many of them richly adorned with gold and precious stones," and arms and shields and "a sort of broad-sword . . . like to hand-swords set with stone [obsidian] knives which cut much better than our very own swords," and bows and arrows stacked to the high ceiling and "artful shields . . . made so that they can be rolled up . . . and quilted cotton armour."

There was a Royal Aviary of which Bernal Díaz said: "I am forced to abstain from enumerating every kind of bird that was there . . . from the royal eagle . . . down to tiny birds of many-coloured plumage . . . from which they take rich plumage that they use in their feather work. All of them bred in these aviaries . . . each kind of bird with its proper food . . . and two hundred men and women to attend them. . . ."

There were the lapidaries, "the skilled jewellers" Moctezuma employed in every craft that was practiced among them, and workers in gold and silver" whose wares even the great gold-smiths in Spain were forced to admire (and Albrecht Dürer, also; see p. 154). "Then those who polished precious stones and jades . . . and the craftsmen in feather-work and painters and sculptors . . . then the Indian women who did the weaving . . . who made such an immense quantity of fine fabrics with wonderful feather-work designs. . . ."

The public markets, of which there were four in the city, were dominated by the great market place at Tlaltelolco, and "we were astounded at the number of people and the quantity of merchandise that it contained and at the good order and control that was maintained. . . . Each kind of merchandise was kept by itself and had its fixed place marked out . . . dealers in gold, silver and precious stones, feather-mantles and embroideries." Then "Indian slaves, both men and women which they brought into the great market for sale as the Portuguese bring Negroes from Guinea, tied to long poles with collars round their necks. Next . . . traders, who sold great pieces of cloth and cotton . . . and those who sold chocolate beans; there was coarse cloth from the maguey fibers, sandals from the plant fiber, another part for those who sold skins of jaguars, pumas, otters, coyotes and deer. . . ."

And "those who sold beans, vegetables, fowls, cocks, turkeys, hares, deer, young dogs"—the eating variety—and every sort of pottery made in a thousand different forms. . . . Those who sold honey and honey paste . . . lumber boards, beams, blocks . . . and the vendors of *ocote*-pine firewood. . . ."

"Truly, my Lord," wrote Hernán Cortés,[26] continuing the description of this fabulous city when eloquence had failed the other, "Truly, my Lord . . . the great city of Tenochtitlán . . . built in the midst of this salt lake, two leagues from any point in the mainland, is connected by four causeways . . . twelve feet wide . . . the city is as large as Seville or Cordova . . . as for the whole, it is so large I am unable to find out exactly the extent of Moctezuma's kingdom. . . ."

All this—to which despite its rather Arabian Nights unreality, archaeology has now fully attested—was what the Spaniards found, a luxuriant form of life of a kind which no other people in the Americas had ever attained.

How had it all come about?

The answer—better the explanation—lies in the cultural history that had long preceded the Aztec.

4. Man Comes to the Americas

No one knows precisely how early it was that man first migrated to the Americas. That man arrived as Man, that he did not grow out of any subhuman present in this continent (there was none) all are in agreement. But how did he arrive? Did he come socially matured, a cultural beast full-blown from the brows of Outer Asia—why, asked Herodotus in irritation, must the continents always be named after women?—casually at one time wandering into it, following the spoor of mammals across that high bourn, the Aleutian land bridge from Outer Mongolia to the Americas; or did he come in a series of migrations over a long period of time from his Asiatic spawning grounds, sufficiently conscious of "something" out there, and continue these treks century upon cen-

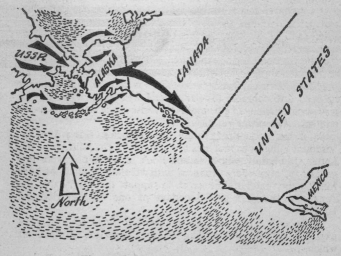

Fig. 6. The origin of man in America.

tury? Or did he come self-propelled in fragile open dugouts across these agitated seas and arrive fully accoutered in cultural panoply to impose himself on his dim-witted cousins earlier arrived?

No one really knows, for the controversy is as old as the discovery of the Americas. The omniscient Church collided at once with reality. If the flood as detailed in the Bible was true, if it destroyed all mankind except Noah and his chosen family to repopulate it, how did these "Americans" get to that continent, and, moreover, who were they? Where theologic logic failed, dialectics was triumphant: the Indians of course were Jews—one of the "lost tribes" of Israel. Labored tracts on this theme, written by the first padres in America, are many.[27] One Fray Diego Durán—the rational part of whose pioneer work in Mexico is used often in this book—wrote that "the supposition is confirmed . . . these natives are of the Ten Tribes of Israel that Salmanassar, King of the Assyrians, made prisoner and carried to Assyria in the time of Hoshea, King of Israel."[28] The Church may have resolved God's anthropology but they had not settled it among the philosophers; the famous Huig de Groot, pioneer of international law, believed in the seventeenth century that the North American Indians were Scandinavian, the Peruvians, Chinese, and the Brazilians, African. He was immediately answered by his countryman Johannes de Laet, who was stirred to great rage over so inept a deduction. Anyone, he wrote, except a dunderpate could see that the American savages were in reality—Scythians. By this time writers of Cromwellian England were involved in the controversy. Thomas Thoroughgood claimed that he had heard from a rabbi in Holland, who had been entertained by a community of Jews in Peru, that the Indians practiced circumcisional rites; that was all the evidence that he needed to compose his pamphlet *Jewes in America*. But he was soon challenged by another, whose tract was engagingly entitled: *Americans no Jewes*.[29]

So it has gone on through the centuries. Edward King, Viscount Kingsborough, was a victim of it. The Church of the Latter Day Saints, whose sacred Book of Mormon traces this genealogy, even today finances with "Golden Tablets of Moroni" highly equivocal research to support the theory that the American Indian is a descendant of one of the tribes of Israel.[30]

Anthropologists would be delighted to have so simple an explanation of the peopling of the Americas; instead of which. . . .

Instead of which there are many theories and of sufficient

variety to fit anyone's wishing. The theory that has long pre-
vailed in anthropological circles is that man came out of Asia
more than 40,000 years ago, abysmally primitive and in the
early neolithic stage* of development, and his culture was by
independent invention in the new "American" land. The
wave of land migrations stopped after climatic change and
after the Bering Strait "land bridge," subject then as now to
constant earthquakes with upheavals and subsidences, finally
sank under Arctic waters.

This theory, upon which archaeological theories pyramided,
is under siege from many quarters; archaeologists, botanists,
geographers have attacked it as untenable. There are fifty
"strikingly similar" features between Pacific island cultures
and those of America, only to be explained by trans-Pacific
diffusions. The "diffusionists" insist that crossings between the
continents, by raft, ship or outrigger, appear to have been
numerous. Even though there is no proof, these theories have
subsisted on the basis of faith, and now in the last years, of
passionate feeling. But a feeling does not adduce its reasons.
It has none; it must be lent to it. There is no positive proof
on either side of the anthropological fence. Arguments,
weighty and frivolous, are many. This has led one British
scientist to the conclusion that "however, the cogency of such
arguments, and there are [good ones] on both sides, is not
generally accepted as convincing and it may be perhaps admitted that the position taken on either side is fortified by
faith. . . ."

However, until someone comes along with facts that can
be weighed in the balance, the American Indian had his cultural beginnings *here*. Early Neolithic man was a land-
wanderer, not a seafarer; he followed the spoor of animals
and he came out of Asia over a land bridge which had been
used for aeons of time by the mammals. So, in keeping with
the opening leitmotif, which allows me to select "according
to my character and idiosyncrasy, at my own taste and fancy
—in a word, as an artist," it came about in this manner:

It was the end of the Ice Age and a new world was forming. The glacial ice that had held the world in eternal winter
was melting and pouring brawling streams of frigid water into
the agitated ocean. Plants that had survived pushed their

---

* The Neolithic or New Stone Age is the period when men began
as food-producers (after 5000 B.C.); before that was the *Mesolithic*,
when he was a hunter and fisher (10,000–4000 B.C.); as *Paleolithic*
man (15,000–10,000 B.C.) he was a food-gatherer and occasional
hunter. All of the early cultures in the "fertile crescent" of the
Near East, Sumerian, Egyptian, etc., were Neolithic.

pallid heads out of the tundra; spores of seeds, wafted on the streams of warmer air, found root, and, under the climatic change, rank luxuriance gradually usurped the place of ice. Over the face of this strange new green earth, after long periods of evolutionary progress, man, *real* man, appeared. He is not out of the pale of world memory; three hundred centuries ago he was making zoömorphic engravings on the walls of caves, creditable intaglios of bison, mammoths, deer, wolves. In body he was a completely formed type; he had wit, ornament and a technique of living. The massive herds of mammals that roamed the earth soon made the acquaintance of this tool-using primate. He followed them, flowing around the Mediterranean and crossing it. He wandered through the wilderness of the Nile into the sylvan lands of India, Java, China, and throughout the whole of Eurasia. Finally he broke into that world-in-itself, Mongolia.

Slow century followed slow century and the metamorphoses of time were making changes in this primitive man—the descendants of the *pithecanthropi* were becoming "race." These Siberian dwellers had black coarse hair and straight, flat, beardless faces with cheekbones in prominence and eyes indexed by the epicanthic fold. They were already, at this time, in the mixo-Neolithic stage of human culture, using stone celts for tools. Some of these then mutated out from

Fig. 7. Aztec warriors, showing their weapons, elaborate headgear (to aid in overawing the enemy), shields and face painting, all part of war equipment.

their world and moved into an utterly new one: forty thousand years ago, these men with the mongoloid eyes, following the northern paths of mammals, made the first invasion of the "Americas."

Primitive man came to America over its roof. Westward from Alaska are twelve hundred miles of islands. The geologic residue of volcanic action, they stretch out in an endless chain across the Bering Sea within sight of outer Siberia. Once they were a land bridge, a connecting link between continents, and over them for countless ages had lapped herds of proto-camels, proto-tapirs and mammoth elephants crossing over from America.

The Ice Age was dominant when this man came to America. We know of his presence, for he has left his bones commingled in fossilized death with extinct animals. Throughout the centuries following this migration, these people moved down the unglaciated Alaskan corridor into the vast land theaters of America. Within five centuries they penetrated the most remote corners of the hemisphere, from ice-bound north to ice-bound south, covering eventually America's entire 135 degrees of latitude. Living here on the shores of frozen or tropical waters, at altitudes varying from sea level to several thousands of feet, living there in forests, grassy plains or deserts; here starved, there in plenty; here with a night of six months' duration, there a night twelve hours long; here among health-giving winds, there cursed with disease—ancient man in America, greatly varying in his cultural milieu, was emerging into a new creature: *Homo Americanus*.

In 5000 B.C. this "American" did not much differ in his cultural accomplishments from primitive man elsewhere. At the time man in the Nile Valley was cultivating millet and barley and laying down the agricultural base upon which Egyptian civilization was to flower, the "American" was selecting the wild plants which would become his maize, potatoes, tomatoes, beans and squash, on which he, too, would build his civilization.

In only one respect—and this an important one for American cultural history—did he differ from the Eurasian. There was no Metal Age: Man here never quit his Neolithic horizon and his tool, although he did invent soft bronze, remained the tool of the *pithecanthropi*, the stone celt.

By the time the Egyptians had reached their cultural apogee and erected the Temple of Amon in 2100 B.C., the Babylonian civilization had come and gone; the legendary Cadmus had left the legacy of the alphabet, and the glory that was to be

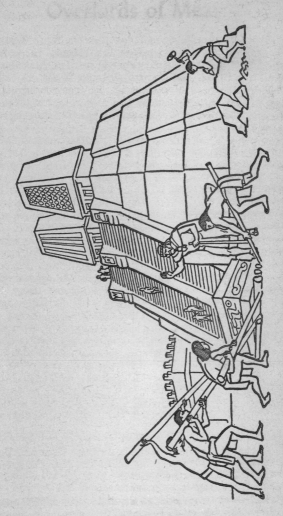

Fig. 8. The building of the principal Aztec pyramid-temple, the *teocalli*, in Mexico-Tenochtitlán. Reconstructed from early Spanish reports, illustrations.

Greece was still contained in societies of Hellenic men abysmally primitive.

In America by that time, the period of great wandering had come to an end; vast spaces of the American earth were menfilled. Out of these cysts of geography cultures came into being. In the hyperborean regions, the Eskimo, flat of face and rotund of body, still lived in the environments of the Ice Age; on the North American plains, tall, keen-eyed tepee dwellers regulated their lives to the biology of the roving animal; farther south, where the caress of the sun was longer, the Indian, becoming partly sedentary, cultivated his plants and under the shelter of rock eaves erected crudely constructed pueblos. At the other extreme of America, the antipodal south, giant Fuegians, their naked bodies wrapped in guanaco skins, walked the frozen tundra, leaving the imprint of their widely spreading feet, "patagones," on the fire-bound land.

In the luxuriant jungles of that same South America, naked Indians with filed teeth hunted man and beast; while west of these dwelling places of the Amazon and the Orinoco was the evening land of the Andes. There in the high, cold, duncolored valleys, a huge-lunged people were developing a great civilization. Around a frigid Andean lake called Titicaca, an Aymara-speaking race had, by the year 1000 B.C., laid down the agricultural patterns that would become Tiahuanacu, while around them and strewn over the rock-hard world, there were many other tribes speaking Quechua, a related language. In time these "Inca" would form all the other Andean tribes into an empire. North of the Inca were the Quitu; north of the Quitu the territory of the Chibcha, whose strange custom of having their "king" wash off his gold-dust-smeared body in a mountain tarn was to create the myth of El Dorado.

Between these two geographic monsters, North and South America, lay Middle America and Mexico, their broken mountains studded with belching volcanoes. They were to be the scene of the great civilizations of ancient America.

Most of Mexico had a homogeneous culture. Whether it was Totonac, Toltec, Zapotec, Huastec, Maya or Aztec, tribe was developed from family; animal diet was supplemented by crude agriculture—plots of ground were burned and seeds inserted in holes made by a fire-hardened stick. Agriculture revolved around corn as the staple, and society was then, as it has remained ever since, machineless. There were no draft animals; the denominator of speed was the foot. Dress was the breechclout; men walked on sandaled feet and women wore a short-petticoated cincture of woven cotton cloth; bare breasts matched bare feet.

In all these tribes society was organized on cognate kinship; the unit was the clan, and each clan had a totemic name. Together these clans became a tribe, bound not by the holding of land, but by the ties of blood. Equally homogeneous was their religion. Belief was animistic: everything in their world, animate or inanimate, possessed "soul," everything was alive, sentient, willful. Gods, both good and evil, had to be propitiated; and art, when it evolved, became dedicated to the metaphysics of this theology. Stoneworking was universal among them. The tides of cultural inheritance ebbed back and forth among all tribes of Mexico and Middle America until that which had been the exclusive cultural property of one tribal kin became the cultural currency of all. There was no later cultural intrusion from either Europe or Asia— or Cambodia. Within itself and by itself, "America" created its own world.

◆
◆
◆

5. Pre-Aztec Cultures

◆
◆
◆

The Tenocha, called "Aztec," were the last to arrive at the Valley of Anáhuac.

In point of historical fact they were so late in becoming the overlords of Mexico that other greater civilizations had already come and gone and were only vague memories in mythology. The sole reason that "Aztec" is so deeply ingrained in history and man's knowing is that it was the dominant political tribute state at the time of the Spanish conquest in 1519, even though its domination was only over a portion of central Mexico. However, when "Aztec" burst upon Europe, it was to be etched deep in human memory. Today's Mexico had then no generic name, and so the name of the island tribute state "Mexico" was imposed upon and over the whole of the land.

It was only much later when the Spanish priest-chroniclers began to question the Indians in regard to their origins and beliefs that they were made aware of the pre-existence of civilizations far, far older and far greater than the Aztec.

Decades of patient archaeological search have now revealed, in the broad, a good deal about these pre-Aztec cultures; with each year scholars are pushing back time. ". . . The earth became our archive," wrote George Vaillant, "the shovel, our reading glass, and in that which nature has eternally destroyed—scattering our materials all over the land," they found and are continuing to find this new archaeological evidence.

By 1000 B.C. the great migrations were over. Peoples filled the fertile lands and were beginning to build temple-cities. In central highland Mexico, throughout the hotlands of Vera Cruz and in the highlands of Guatemala, they laid down their city-centers. Man became sedentary; he had developed agriculture and he knew leisure. During the same period in the "other lands," the Phoenicians were devising the alphabet, the Greek-Dorians were arriving in the Peloponnesus, and Europe, thinly populated, was coming out of raw savagery.

36

One tribe was already evident: the Olmec (800 B.C.–A.D. 600?), who lived in the hotlands of Vera Cruz and Tabasco; 800 B.C. marks the beginning of the pre-classic period in Mexico.

It was long suspected that the Olmec would prove to be one of the earlier cultures and now radio-carbon dating from the Olmec site at La Venta has confirmed the evidence that Olmec structures "appear to have been constructed and used during . . . four centuries . . . 800–400 B.C." [31]

In Aztec mytho-history, the Olmec were known as "the people-who-live-in-the-direction-of-the-rising-sun" [32] and a glyph history of them shows that their paradisiacal "wealth" consisted of rubber, pitch, jade, chocolate and bird feathers. We do not know what they called themselves. "Olmec" derives from *Olli* (rubber); their symbol, often seen, is that of the tree of life, the "weeping wood." They traded rubber and

Fig. 9. Olmec culture, symbolized by the great stone heads with thick lips and broad nostrils, found in the hotlands of Vera Cruz and Tabasco. The Olmec culture dates back to and beyond 800 B.C.

they presumably made the rubber balls used for the game called *tlachtli*. A talented and mysterious people, they appeared as early as 1000 B.C. along the Isthmus of Tehuantepec (where the waist of Mexico is slender and level between the two oceans), but they were particularly centered about the Coatzacoalco River basin on the Gulf coast. For untold centuries burial mounds and pyramids built by them lay covered by the jungle; in these archaeologists have found carved jade, sensitively modeled clay figurines "of an unprecedented high artistic quality," [33] says the late Miguel Covarrubias.

In only recent times have the great Olmec stone heads been unearthed, by Dr. Matthew Stirling. [34] At Tres Zapotes he found one colossal head, seven feet high, flat-nosed and sensually thick-lipped. The carving is sensitive and realistic; the style is found among no other people and once seen will never be forgotten or confused with any other. Other colossal heads have been found; in similar style there are carved masks, heads in smaller scale, and votive axes, all exhibiting the same squat figures with perforated noses, pronounced mongoloid features, and narrow slits for eyes. These have been found in widely scattered areas. The Olmec large-scale monuments, however, are found mostly between Vera Cruz, Tabasco, highland Guatemala and Oaxaca—this is definite Olmec land. A *stela* found at Tres Zapotes and numbered by the bar and dot system, bears what is by far the earliest recorded "American" date: 31 B.C.

Only now are Olmec structural complexes coming into focus. They had temple-cities, erected stone *stelae* to mark the flight of time or to commemorate important events; the stepped pyramid, the courtyard, the *tlachtli* ball game, were all cultural features in general use. The Olmec still occupied their traditional tropic-land when the Spanish first arrived. There is no record of them beyond the observation that they tattooed their bodies, inlaid their teeth with jade, flattened their heads, plucked their face hair, hunted heads for trophies, flaying the skin and tanning them as the Jivaro in the Upper Amazon did the *tzantza*. They practiced circumcision and as penance drew blood from their penis. [35]

The art of the Olmec is unique—simple, direct, forceful. There is nothing quite like it in all Mexico. Yet aside from this "art" they must have been possessed of certain social dynamics to stamp their pattern on Mexico's cultural history.

The Maya (1500 B.C.–A.D. 1537), who appeared early, had a great influence over the development of culture in Mexico and were the longest-lived. For what length of time they built their temple-cities before their first calendar was set up is not known. The earliest *stela*, at Uaxcatun, is dated

A.D. 416, later by 477 years than the first recorded Olmec date.

From the earliest times there was much cultural interchange among all these peoples. A large trading area at Xicalango in Tabasco was the Maya contact center for the outside world where, under terms of peace, things of their lands were exchanged with Central Mexico. Within a large traditional tribal land the Maya, free of any large-scale outside invasion until the twelfth century, perfected their calendar, glyph writing, and stone carving, and evolved the complex temple cities which can still be seen today. Their influence on the other cultures in the high Mexican plateaus was very marked.

Monte Albán (500 B.C.–A.D. 1522), a ceremonial center and temple-city, lies in Oaxaca atop high treeless hills overlooking the valley and the present-day Spanish city of the same name. One of the oldest in Mexico, its occupation continued from the earliest preclassic period, perhaps as early as 1000 B.C., until the coming of the Spaniard in 1522. This immense time period of 2,500 years is divided into five archaeological horizons. Its beginnings are shrouded in mystery. Dr. Alfonso Caso, who first uncovered it and has worked on its problems continuously for twenty years, believes that its formal structures date as far back as 500 B.C. Even as early as this they had already developed glyph writing, a calendar and a complete cosmogony.

Who were the early builders? From the beginning it seems it was a city, although not habitable, of the gods, visited by men and women alike. Before the city (its original name is unknown) took on its Zapotec character, it had from the earliest times a temple with a frieze of dancing figures done in the Olmec style, a "powerful and mysterious archaism of expressive monsters." These Olmec-styled figures and *stelae,* with the still undecipherable glyphs, are the primary mystery of Monte Albán.

One will grasp how really early all this was if one remembers that in the same period of world history Nebuchadnezzar was destroying Jerusalem and carrying off the Jews to their first slavery; Cyrus, king of the Persians, was on the loose and the whole Middle East was in an expansion mood; by the time the people of Mexico were beginning to set up their temple-city states, Xerxes had conquered Egypt and was setting off to invade Greece. Although the "Americans" had none of the stimulation of the "fertile crescent" of the Near East—which brought the wheel, iron and the alphabet to the world—they were advanced in city planning, writing and sculpture.

Fig. 10. Zapotec art, which centered about Monte Albán, is typified by this funeral ceramic.

At about A.D. 300 Monte Albán moved into a transition period, threw off its Maya influence and turned to its own sources—the Zapotec. For the four hundred years that followed, the great plaza was enlarged and temples, pyramids, ball courts and the frescoed tombs were constructed.

The Mixtec (668*–1521), whose capital city was Cholula

* This date was reached by Covarrubias by deducting the 500 years of Olmec occupation of Mixtec land, mentioned by Juan de Torquemada in his *Monarquía Indiana* (Madrid, 1723), from the date of 1168, when the Olmec were driven from Cholula.

Fig. 11. Mixtec art forms resemble the Aztec. Mixtec civilization, beginning as early as 700 B.C., was centered about Cholula. The illustration is taken from a part of a Mixtec codex, an origin-myth.

(the present-day Puebla), occupied a geographical buffer zone between the coast and the highland; it was subject to all the recurring waves of conquest, first from the coast (Olmec), then from the highlands (Toltec). Later they became conquerors; after 1350 they extended south into Monte Albán, only in turn to be overrun by the Aztec after 1450.

The Mixtec have wondrous tales to tell of themselves. The Indian noble Ixtililoxochitl writing in the seventeenth century told of giants and Olmec and much about the pyramid to the Plumed Serpent, the greatest in all the Americas.[36] Quetzalcoatl was a mysterious figure through all Mexico and Yucatan. That he once lived can be assumed (later rulers of the Toltec took his patronymic just as Moslem rulers today carry the name of their prophet or Romans "Caesar"). It is difficult to separate man from myth. Quetzalcoatl was a demiurge, priest and ruler, conceived by virginal birth years after his father's death (his mother was made pregnant when she swallowed a piece of jade); he was ruler of the Toltec for twenty-two years. He lived in Tula, lost a civil war,* fled with a good-sized Toltec force, reached the Coatzacoalcos River on the day of 2-Reed in Aztec reckoning (the sign under which he was born), and set sail into the open sea with the prophecy that he would again return on the recurrence of that date.

He left his impress on the Mixtec, who, like the others in this high cultural period, had writing and paper (some Mixtec codices survive). They were advanced in the arts of building and in agricultural and social planning, and, despite wars of rapine and conquest, their cultural influence lasted over thousands of years; they greatly influenced the Aztec.

The Huastec (500 B.C.–A.D. 1521), who occupied northern Vera Cruz and extended inland as well to include highland Mexico (now the states of Tamaulipas, San Luis Potosí, Hidalgo and Querétaro), have lately also been determined to have been one of the earlier cultures,[37] enduring in more or less continued activity for 2,000 years and silenced only by the arrival of the Spanish. The distinctive art forms of the Huastec have been known for many decades but it is only in the last fifteen years that Huastec architecture has been uncovered.[38]

The Totonac, "discovered" by the collectors of modern art because of their non-objective art styles, also appeared during

---

* What perhaps was a real political struggle for power between two concepts of government—the peace-loving "positive" Quetzalcoatl against the "negative" Teccatlipoca, "Smoking Mirror," who brought the terror—was rationalized to "correlate historical events with an older mythus."

the preclassic period. The Totonac had, so far as it is known, an uninterrupted cultural continuity in central Vera Cruz from approximately 500 B.C. until the arrival in 1519 of Hernán Cortés. They formed a sort of linguistic "sandwich" between the Olmec and the Huastec, who were of Maya stock and speech. Totonac country has yielded for many decades some of the "finest and most sophisticated specimens of Indian art" [39]—the freehand clay figurines always in laughter; the "laughing heads" and life-sized stone heads attached to a tenon, meant to be placed in walls as an architectonic motif; the strange U-shaped objects as large as horse-collars and resembling them in size and shape, carved from polished green or black stone, exquisitely decorated and made for an unknown purpose. This art, gay, sybaritic, a contrast to the austere Maya or Aztec form, is a Totonac characteristic. They also left behind an impressive number of temple-cities which, although covered by jungle and eroded by the centuries, still remain morphous, so that Mexican archaeologists are able to restore them. All this culture which had been nurturing for a thousand years was at the disposal of the Aztec.

In the valley of Anáhuac, in the central Mexican plateau, after 200 B.C., the Toltec learned better management of their

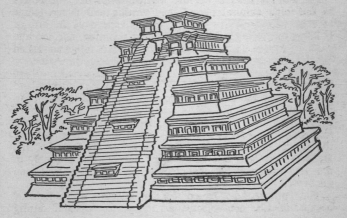

Fig. 12. Totonac architecture is typified by the temple of Tajín at Papantla in Vera Cruz. The niches held small idols, the temple was atop the pyramid. The Totonac began as far back as 500 B.C. They were a functional tribe in full flower when Cortés arrived in 1519.

agriculture and produced a social surplus. With that, Teotihuacán came into being.

Toltec-Teotihuacán (200 B.C.–A.D. 900), "Place of the Gods," thirty-two miles northwest of Mexico City, dwarfs in magnitude all else in Mexico and Middle America (save perhaps Tikal in Guatemala); the remains of the great ceremonial city alone cover an area of eight square miles. It challenges the imagination how the Toltec at so early a period could have marshaled so many people—with enough leisure, unoccupied with their fight about the feeding trough—to build and maintain so enormous a religious center. So renowned was Teotihuacán that it served as model for all subsequent temple-cities, and the Toltec remained—even when monuments were covered and were only a vague memory—the Master Builders,

Fig. 13. Toltec-Teotihuacán was the classic culture of the valley of Mexico. It endured from 100 B.C. until A.D. 900. The symbol of Quetzalcoatl—a serpent's head wreathed in quetzal plumes— is Toltec.

and thereafter all artisans who were masters, especially painters and *tlacuilo*-writers, were called "Toltec" even down into Aztec times.

The history of these Toltec, less vague when read in the light of recent archaeological findings, is found in the *Annals of Cuauhtitlan;* later, less speculative, literature [40] and further exploration and excavation have filled in the gaps. The Toltec spun in cotton, which means that they maintained contact with the hotlands, as cotton does not grow in the high plateau; men had thicker garments for cold weather and women dressed in loose-fitting *huipillis* and wrap-around skirts; warriors wore (as did the Aztec one thousand years later) quilted cotton armor; their weapons were as the Aztec; and their priests, as did the Aztec, went about filthily in black unwashed tunics that swept the ground. Their chiefs dressed as did the common man, only more elaborately, and they were monogamous. In their houses the Toltec constructed the *temascal* steam bath, a common feature among the Aztec.

When Toltec history emerges through the myths that surround it, it follows a pattern. A priest-astrologer guided them through Mexico until they found a fertile valley. There they built their city of Tollan or Tula. The chronology of their kings, which must have been chanted for centuries, was etched into the memory-pattern, so that when repeated to a double-languaged scribe and set down in the sixteenth century, it gave the names of their rulers. It told of Toltec dominance under their eighth ruler, a rule which embraced all the land between Jalisco to the north and Cuernavaca to the south; it told of the elaborate ritual of their polytheistic religion and it mentioned in detail the woman known as *Xochitl* (pronounced *sho-chitl*), who made popular the beverage now called *pulque* by fermenting the juice of the maguey plant.

Like their rivals of the same period, the Toltec of Teotihuacán had ideographic writing, tribal records, *amatl*-paper books which pictured their bewildering cosmogony; they also had the 52-year cycle, magical *tonal-pohualli* (the numeration of fate), a system of prognostication based on a period of 260-day count, and a lunar calendar for everyday use. And they built the awe-inspiring temple-city Teotihuacán.

Teotihuacán endured from 200 B.C., the approximate time of its shadowy and tenuous beginnings, until about A.D. 900. Its period of slow decline is revealed in its pottery. Here is reflected the gradual change that came over a tribe that lost its political power but kept its respect among others. Another tribe, the Chichimec, moved into the Toltec domain and took up the remains of "empire" but found themselves swallowed up in the chaos between the years 1100 and A.D. 1300 that followed the break-up of the "age of cultural unity." [41] Meanwhile the Toltec, now migratory, developed two other cultural areas, Tula and Xochicalco.

Tula (900–A.D. 1116) was built at the apogee of Toltec power, and is of the greatest importance. What was once regarded as pure mythology—promoting an ironical remark by one writer about the "vague science of anthropology and the exact art of myth"—has in many instances been confirmed by archaeology about this fabulous Tula, with its immense statuary and temples. The very close resemblance of its architecture to the cities of Mayapan, principally Chichén Itzá in Yucatan, confirms the trek of the Toltec to that region in the twelfth century. Is this Tula, the legendary "Tollan" as described by the padre-chronicler Sahagun, the beautiful city "of rich palaces of green jade and white and red shell, where the ears of corn and pumpkins reached the size of a man, where cotton grew in the plant in all colours and the air was always filled with rare birds of precious feathers . . ."? If Tula is Tollan, eight centuries have changed the land. It is now dry, parched, dust-filled, no "precious bird" in its right avian mind would go there, and yet. . . .

And yet the description of the city is not as mythical as first believed. Archaeologists found elaborately carved and painted walls, a stepped pyramid with the remains of a temple at its summit, with the symbol of Quetzalcoatl—two stone-painted serpents fifteen feet high acting as caryatids for the elaborate façades of the temple; carved pillars for the temple of the warriors; immense stone-carved figures; and that sculptural idea which traveled farthest, the reclining figure of Chac-mool looking blankly into space and holding a stone tray on which palpitating human hearts were placed as food for the gods. This same frightening figure, without any change, was to be carved and set up in the capital of the Aztec, and was to find its way 1,000 miles south into Yucatan.

Xochicalco (700–A.D. 1200), of Toltec origin or influence, with its famous temple to the Plumed Serpent, was built more or less at the same time as Tula (A.D. 900). Lying lonely in the sun on top of bare hills, not more than twenty direct miles south of Cuernavaca (off the main road to Taxco and the Pacific), it was one of the first "ruins" to enter literature, having been explored by Padre Alzate in 1777 and illustrations of it published in 1810 by Alexander von Humboldt.

Xochicalco, "The Place of Flowers," was a ceremonial, perhaps administrative, center for the tribes which lived in

Fig. 14. Tula is Toltec. The fabuolus city, north of Mexico, is presumed to have been built between A.D. 900–1100 and ruled by Quetzalcoatl. Many Toltec architectural forms are found at Chichén Itzá in Yucatan.

this region (state of Morelos). It is situated on the highest hills, looks down upon two fresh-water lakes two miles distant, fish-filled, with much game and a fertile country and in a strongly fortified position. The hills were artificially flattened and terraced with strong points for defense. Four roads coming from the four cardinal directions led into the principal plaza, where the temple to Quetzalcoatl stands. The Aztec knew of it and were influenced by it.

All the cultures listed here—and there are many more—were established on Mexican soil as long as 2,500 years before the Aztec made their appearance as an organized tribe. By the time they put in their appearance close on to A.D. 1200, the tides of these earlier cultures had swept back and forth across the face of the land, devastating one and the other, at the same time developing all the varied aspects of much of that which we call civilization. And to all this the Aztec were the heirs.

II

THE PEOPLE

◆◆◆◆◆◆◆◆◆◆◆◆◆◆◆◆◆◆◆◆◆◆◆◆◆◆◆◆◆◆◆◆◆◆◆◆◆

6. The Origins of the Aztec

The "Aztec" came into Anáhuac, the valley of Mexico, in
A.D. 1168. This, recorded in their written ideographic histories,
has been synchronized with our calendar; no one has cast
doubt on it.

The Tenocha-Aztec were wanderers, a landless "wanting"
tribe who came out of the north of Mexico (some hold from
America's southwest but there is no evidence of it); they
were of Nahuatl speech, that language which was also the
speech of the Toltec. The Aztec were of the "have-nots,"
moved about, settling here briefly, wandering there, nibbling

Fig. 15. Aztec temples and houses, with a chieftain in march
toward them. Footprints indicate migration or movement. Redrawn from the Aztec codices.

at the nether edge of another's lands until a battle ensued; then peregrination began all over again. The date 1168, to be sure, does not tell us with certainty that the Aztec settlement in Mexico began then, but only, as Dr. Vaillant believed, that at that time the Aztec, who were then cultural nonentities, had begun to use a calendar which had been in general use for 1,000 years. [42] Who were the Aztec and from whence— it is answered in their mythico-histories.* Like all other such origin myths, these differ in detail, not in basic content. The Inca came out of caves; Greeks were given divine guidance by an *autologos* in a darkened sanctuary; Christian myths overflow with heavenly-inspired grottoes. And so the Aztec. They found in a cave the Hummingbird Wizard, the famous Huitzilopochtli (a name the conquistadors never mastered, calling it *Huichilobos,* "Witchy-wolves"). The idol gave them advice. It sounded well: wander, look for lands, avoid any large-scale fighting, send pioneers ahead, have them plant maize, when the harvest is ready move up to it; keep me, Huitzilopochtli, always with you, carrying me like a banner, feed me on human hearts torn from the recently sacrificed. . . . All of which the Aztec did.

The number, even approximate, of the Tenocha tribe at that time we do not know. It was minuscule—perhaps 1,000, perhaps 5,000, not much more. At least in so thickly settled an area as the valley of Anáhuac, they were so insignificant that their arrival at the lakes passed completely unnoticed and there is no record of their arrival in the stately forest of Chapultepec for a generation, from 1250 A.D. All this is understandable. No one regarded as "historical" the internal events of other tribes. History was perpendicular, not horizontal; it had no cross-references. During these "wandering years," the Aztec were absorbing the culture of their neighbors. They grew. They made enemies. They expanded. Their clans being too small for wife-yield, they took to wife-stealing, and now for the first time their neighbors around the valley took cognizance. They were set upon. One part of the tribe was swept into servitude, another escaped to one of the swampy islets out in Lake Texcoco. Those left behind were involved in the wars of their captors, wherein they displayed such valor that when asked to name a boon, they asked for the daughter of the chieftain, so that through her they could

* The word "Aztec" as applied to the Tenocha is not of certain origin. They said that they came from some fabled land *Aztlan;* because of this the Spaniards referred to them as Az-tec; of a certainty they neither called themselves that nor were they called that before the Conquest.

form a respectful lineage. It was granted, but they sacrificed the beautiful girl, flayed her and draped the skin over their head-priest so that he might impersonate the Nature Goddess. When the chieftain of their captors, the father of the girl, arrived in gorgeous array, he expected naturally to attend a wedding ceremony. Instead he found—this. One can somehow understand his wrath. Those Tenocha who escaped the butchery by his warriors fled and joined their tribesmen on the second islet on the lake.

Tenochtitlán, the island city-state, became an entity and began historically in 1325. The lakes wherein the incipient Aztec capital lay, and as shapeless as free-swimming protoplasm, were five,* situated in the valley of Anáhuac, a level plain over 7,000 feet in altitude. From the high snow-covered mountains that surrounded it there poured the brawling streams that made these lakes, which were 50 miles long, 500 square miles in surface, and ringed with tall, slender marsh grass. The lakes were deep at some parts but shallow in others, especially so about the islets that formed the city of the Tenochas. The exigencies of the moment called first for housing. Wattle and daub houses thatched with the marsh grass came first. At a later date, 4-Coatl (1325), the Tenocha dedicated their first temple. In the beginning, and by agreement with the tribes that ringed the shore, they had permission to use border lands for planting. This land they augmented with *chinampa*-agriculture, a process by which they made outsized wickerwork oval-shaped baskets, which then were towed to their islets, anchored to the shallow bottom and filled with earth. In these they grew their crops. Mexico-Tenochtitlán thus was hand-fashioned.

During the years 1403-55 (Aztec III period) the growing city-state, through alliance and war, depressions and recovery, outgrew the primitive stage and filled in the background with new and enlarged cultural horizons. Thereafter the Aztec took the center of the Mexican stage and became the principal directors of life within and without the valley of Anáhuac. So they expanded as all peoples expand, as life itself lives, at the expense of other lives and at the expense of other peoples; this is reasonable, understandable and natural.

Techniques moved slowly. Metal working came up from South America by slow stages through indirect trade, arrived in Mexico about the eleventh century. Although advanced in many ways, these "Americans" were yet without the wheel,

* Contiguous and with five names: Chalco and Xochimilco were fresh-water; Texcoco brackish; the most northern, Xalcocan and Zumfango, very salty.

the rotary quern and draft animals. Mexico in 1519, as has been said, "was where Sumer and Egypt stood in 3500 B.C."; the picture, however, is not that clear.

At the same historical moment—A.D. 1100—that the Inca in Peru were emerging from a similarly obscure position to became a real empire,[43] the Aztec were, by the same imperialistic means, evolving as the overlords of Mexico.

So, within these extreme dates of 1168–1521, the Tenocha called "Aztec" came into their own.

7. Appearance: What Manner of Men

The base of Aztec society was the plebe—the *macehualli* or common Indian.

While his place was less that of an automaton than mere man under the Inca empire, where he was only a "head-count," still he was, in labor terms, both rank and file. *Macehua* derived from "to suffer" or "to earn merits"—in reality he did both. He was a member of a clan and part of an earth-cell, of a sort of mutual-aid society; he was, in summary, an able-bodied, tax-paying Indian. First and foremost he was a farmer, in European terms a peasant, and, in the still highly valid expressions of Oswald Spengler [44] "the eternal man, independent of every culture . . . one who pre-

Fig. 16. The Aztec warrior-farmer, called *macehualli*. As plebe he was the base of Aztec society. These figures, redrawn from the *Codice Mendocino*, show two aspects of his life—as farmer and as warrior.

ceded it, he outlived it, a dumb creature propagating himself from generation to generation, limited to soil-bound callings and aptitudes, with a mystical, dry, shrewd understanding that sticks to practical matters."

Yet this common Aztec was something more. He was also a warrior, part of an agrarian militia. As the common Roman was a worker-soldier, so the common *macehualli* (plural: *macehualtin*) must be understood as a farmer-warrior.

Like most of the indigenes in Mexico, he was short—between 5 feet 1 and 5 feet 5—broad-headed and thickset. Tireless, he was used to walking since childhood and could carry a load of 75 pounds, fifteen hours a day. His arms were long and feet broad in proportion to his height; his gait straight and inclined to be "pigeoned"; the arches, as one can see in Aztec drawings of footsteps, were very high and fully arched.

The head was characterized by the jet-black eyes, lidded with the "epicanthic fold," which gives the eye an almond shape. The hair was dark, coarse, abundant, except on his body and face. He was relatively beardless, and face hair was deemed objectionable, so that mothers used tweezers to pluck it out and applied hot cloths to stifle the hair follicles. They were "beardless," even though Cortés said that the Tlascalans had "barbers to shave you." The Aztec face was further made prominent by a hooked "Roman nose" (although any citizen of that *imperium* would have been shocked at so odious a comparison) which grew more so in old age. Their color varied from dark to light brown; the face could assume a fierce mien and often great dignity, an expression they carried into battle or palaver.

And in addition to the epicanthic fold that betrayed his Asian origin, there was the Mongolian spot. This does not seem to have appeared with high frequency among the Aztec, yet it is prominent even today among the Maya; it is an irregular-shaped spot, blue to purple in color, varying in size from a small coin to a dinner plate, and located at the base of the spine; it is very obvious in young females, disappears with age. The same characteristic is found throughout Asia.

Aztec women were naturally smaller (4 feet 8), and delicate. Yet it was a false frailty. They bore children quickly, often in the milpa-fields; they followed their men on long marches (the women attached to the Mexican army in recent times were part of the quartermaster corps), and carried their share of the load, including the inevitable baby. Many of them were of striking appearance; the Spaniards thought so, married them and found them attractive. Doña Marina, "The Tongue," an Indian girl who helped talk the Spaniards into victory over Moctezuma, was declared to be an "excellent woman . . . full of grace."

Dress was, for the common man, simple and expedient; the same raiment was worn night and day. All wore the loincloth (*maxtlatl*), a cincture that was passed between the legs and brought about the waist, its two ends hanging in front and back and usually embellished. In this he worked on marches where he carried cargo. The mantle (*tilmantli*) —in today's usage, the *manta*—was a rectangular piece of woven cloth tied over one shoulder, made at first from the coarse fibers of the maguey (*ixtle*) and later, when contact with the hotlands was general, from cotton. They used neither buttons nor pins. When the *tilmantli* was sufficiently flowing, it covered the whole body when seated. Many of these often were beautifully woven; of this however we have little or no evidence except their own pictures and the descriptions by their conquerors. The common Indian mostly walked with naked feet until he grew in social importance; then he traveled in sandals (*cactli*) made from animal skin or maguey fibers. For the chieftain or demigod, they were of gold.

Fig. 17. Aspects of Aztec cookery. In the upper left, *camotli* (sweet potatoes); to the right is the stone *metate* on which corn is ground. The woman cooks red peppers on a *cumal,* and in the lower right-hand corner newly baked corncakes are covered to retain freshness.

Hair styles had some variation: in everyday use the hair hung in bangs and was cut in back by barbers with an obsidian knife—"Pagankopf" the Germans would call it—or it was let grow long and was braided into a thick "pigtail." When at war it was decorated with two turkey or eagle feathers.

Woman's dress in this plebe class, while of only one cut, varied greatly in design, color and pattern, for women were the principal weavers. The woman wore an underskirt (*cueitl*) of ankle length and often magnificently embroidered; when abroad she would put over this a poncho-like dress (*huipilli*), a rectangular piece of cloth with a slit through which the head passed, the sides sewn except for armholes—a prosaic description of some of the finest weaving in pattern and color found in the continent, which Bernal Díaz, then an impressionable young man of twenty-three, found "rich and beautifully ornamented." Her sandals, lighter than those used by men, she wore only on journeys or if her social position demanded it. Her hair, long and lustrous and black, grew to full length; it was braided with ribbons for festival days, allowed to hang when about the house; it was gathered and wrapped about the crown of the head when she worked in the fields. Cosmetics were used, mostly by those of the "directing classes" or courtesans (*auianime*) and even sometimes by women of the common sort when at the markets things touched their souls. Unguents, perfumes and creams were available.[45]

8. The Traffic of Speech

Nahuatl (pronounced "*nah*-wah-t'l") was the language of the Aztec.

It was neither their invention nor their perfection, since it was spoken by Toltec, Chichimec and numerous other tribes. It became, however, the lingua franca of Mexico and Central America (just as Quechua was that of the Inca in Peru) because of the conquest by the Aztec, the penetration of his merchants and trade. And when later reduced to Spanish orthography, a further extension of it was made by the Church, which used it and translated the Christian catechism and other religious manuals into it, thus enlarging its speaking arena.

Nahuatl is one of the eight families of Uto-Aztecan stock. More detailed studies have been made of it, especially of Aztec, than of "any other American linguistic family." [46] This has been mostly because of the late B. L. Whorf, who was, en passant, a non-professional. Nahuatl speech is related to some of the language phyllomes of the Southwest Indians (Pima, Shoshoni, Sonora), hence the belief among some that the Aztec were a fighting breed out of this region. There are seven hundred languages in Mexico; Nahuatl, which was somewhat confined to the central plateau but expanded following the Aztec conquest, belongs to one of the five large phyla of Macro-Penutian speech. Studies of it are highly specialized and its students use technical terms among themselves and in their publications which are never used in normal communications. If a layman were to read the one on "The origin of the Aztec '-tl' "—a suffix which the reader will find often in these pages—he would be as bewildered as Alice in her Wonderland when she came upon the "smile without the cat."

Nahuatl is a living language. Thousands still speak it, there are books and musical records in it, some of Mexico's foremost scholars converse in it; it is very graphic and plastic, as will be seen when the Aztec natural plant classification is discussed. The language was as compounded as the Aztec ideographic writing and capable of expressing great feeling and poetry, and although the early Spaniards found the suffix "-tl" very bewildering, sixteenth-century savants who mastered the tongue found it clear and harmonious, with an extended vocabulary.

Although there is no space here for a discussion of Aztec grammar, it had all the traffic of language—what one writer has called "accidence, the table manners of speech." Our modern grammar did not begin much before the Reformation; before that there was a cheerful indifference to syntax and spelling. Therefore it is amazing to find any people so removed as were the American Indians from the web of Old World communications yet developing so involved a speech and grammar. There were derivative words and fusion "arising from context and pronunciation without regard to meaning"; agglutination was its natural result. What additions the Aztec made to his inherited speech Nahuatl is not known, yet it must have been substantial because, as a result of their conquests, new things were pouring into their world and they had to have some fixed grammar to receive them, with flexions of person and tense. One of the first books printed in Mexico (1555) was Motolinía's *Vocabulario*. . . . Grammars, catechisms, translations of texts from ideographic Nahuatl into Spanish orthography, have followed century after century until now there is quite enough for a serious study on *Aztec Literature*.[47]

The speech of the Aztec *macehualli* had the same earthiness as the soil-man's everywhere; practical and with careless speech habits his words grew out of that usage of needs which is the living morphology of any language. Ordinary men were careless about the meaning of an affix, of the flexions of person, number, case, gender; but in the *calmecac* schools of Mexico-Tenochitlán where good Nahuatl speech was taught, corrected, extended, so that high-placed persons could speak properly to the gods or impress visiting chieftains, this traffic of speech was carefully studied. It must have been. Those informants who worked with the first Spaniards in setting it down *knew* the grammar of their speech. This example will suffice; when Sahagun in 1529 began to take down the remembered sagas of the Aztec, this is how he gave it in Nahuatl, using his own orthography, about the Sun, the principal god-year:

> Tonatiuh [sun] quautlevanitl
> xippilli, nteutl [god]
> tone, tlaextia motonameyotia,

Fig. 18. The dance of *Xocotl-huetzi*. This took place in the month of that name, which celebrated the "fall of fruits." Men danced about a tree ornamented with paper flags.

tontoqui, tetlati, tetkaati, teytoni, teixtlileuh,
teixtlilo, teixcaputzo, teixtlecaleuh.

The sun, eagle, dart of fire,
Prince of the year, God
illuminates, makes things glow, lights them with
   its rays,
is warm, burns people, makes them perspire,
   turns dark the
countenance of people, blackens them, makes
   them black as smoke.[48]

One said much in Nahuatl with little. And while the language
was by no means as far-flung geographically as Quechua in
Peru, which spread for the same reasons—i.e., conquest from
Chile to Colombia, the Aztec speech penetrated far enough
—from Mexico down to Nicaragua.

9. The Clan-Aztec Holding Corporation

All—or almost all—of early native American societies were democratic.

There was rank without class. The community, not the individual, owned the land, and most decisions were made by popular ballot, as, for example, by the American Plains Indians. Or done in the manner which Tacitus described in writing of how the Germans came to decisions in the depths of their forests: "When the mass is to decide they take their seats fully armed . . . silence is then demanded . . . such hearing is given to king or chief as age, rank, military distinction or eloquence can secure . . . if a proposal displeases them, the people roar out their dissent; if they approve, they clash their spears." [49]

When once the Indian began to sustain himself wholly from agriculture, he became a member of a commune. This could be a clan or sib (kin, related by blood) as among the Plains Indians, replete with totem or badge (as a coat of arms that identified), or an *ayllu* among the Inca, or it could be a *calpulli* (from *calli*, house) as it was among the Aztec. Most of the indigenous American communes were based on this type of organization, a clan as an economic unit united by supernatural (i.e., blood) bonds.

An Indian was born into a clan or *calpulli*. A *calpulli* was a group of houses of extended families. This clan owned certain lands which it held communally. A married man was loaned his piece of land directly from the clan. No one had title to the land he worked, he was allowed only the produce of it; if he died without issue or the land was neglected or he was "drummed out" of his clan, the piece reverted back to the holding corporation. So exact were some of these, that records were kept on *amatl*-paper of the various land tracts along with a rebus drawing of the holder's name. According to their records there were seven original *calpulli*; once they settled on their island-state, Tenochtitlan, these were enlarged into twenty.

Each of these owned, or held by treaty, land on the mainland. At first agricultural land was very limited; when a *calpulli* had none, its members industriously made *chinampas*, the so-called "floating gardens." These were the reed-woven baskets, eight feet in diameter, filled with earth and anchored in the shallow waters. Roots penetrating the basket bottom eventually firmly fixed them to the lake bottom. By this laborious method, a *calpulli* could enlarge its produce and extend its clan holdings. Yet as their war conquests proceeded and more alien tribes were forced to yield terrain on the mainland, land grew plentiful and was divided proportionately among all the clans that formed the Aztec tribe. This system of land tenure was, as V. Gordon Childe calls it, " the fatal limitation of . . . Neolithic economy . . . the sole outlet for an expanding population was to annex more land for cultivation and suitable land was not unlimited." [50]

The Aztec clan system was not as rigid as the Peruvian system of the *ayllu*, which was overorganized. Yet it was so arranged that the whole group-family, the *calpulli*, moved as a social unit. "Mexican society," observed Dr. Vaillant, "existed for the benefit of the tribe and each member was supposed to do his part in preserving the community." [51]

An Indian born into a clan could not lose his clan rights nor his right to a piece of clan-held land, of a size sufficient to feed the numbers in his family; no one except the duly elected clan chieftains could force an Indian to forfeit these rights by expulsion for crime or other anti-social acts.

10. Marriage—"The Tying of the *Tilmantli*"

Tied together—"spliced," in the Menckenian American colloquial—was not merely a figure of speech in Aztec society. Marriage was symbolized by the actual tying together of the edges of the *tilmantli* cloaks of bride and groom, and once so joined, they were supposed to be "hitched" for life.

A man married at twenty, a girl at about sixteen. There was not in this society a prohibition against bachelors as there was among the Inca. But economic factors and especially the preparation of food made it impossible for a man to live without a woman—corncakes, the irreplaceable staff of life, made twice daily, took two hours for each preparation and this was a woman's task.

Fig. 19. Marriage—"the tying of the *tilmantli*." An illustration from the *Codice Mendocino* depicts Aztec marriage customs. A man and woman, tied together, listen to homilies delivered by the old women who were the marriage-brokers.

Marriage was outside the clan, for since all clan members were considered to be of the same blood, to marry within it would be incestuous. Marriage was exogamous and it had a formality more complex than ours. A young man who contemplated marriage had to consult with the clan council. While sexual attraction and affection played a part, they knew then as now that one does not only marry the woman, one also marries the family. In this case it was more than a family contract, it was a social contract, for by it one's child inherited the birthright of entrance into a clan.

Old women were the marriage brokers. There exists a curious ideographic picture history, a sort of comic-book history, of the whole proceedings in the *Codice Mendocino*.[52] While love was doubtlessly a determinant in courtship, it was not strongly emphasized. There were too many tabus. Rémy de Gourmont felt that one must associate the ideas of pleasure with the idea of love if one wants to understand anything of the movement of life. Yet it is also true that there occurs in neither Aztec nor Maya pantheons a "goddess of love" nor are there drawings or pottery showing acts of generation such as exist among the Mochica or Chimu in Peru, and no drawing of the ithyphallic. Aldous Huxley compared their art of love unfavorably with the Hindu: "There is no sex in the art of the Maya [and the Aztec] but by way of compensation, what a lot of death. . . ." He thought that the climate and diseases of the climate might have had something to do with it. "It is difficult to make love on an empty stomach and still more difficult to make it with an intestine full of ankylostoma."[53]

On the night of marriage the bride was carried to the groom's house on the back of the old woman matchmaker. All the principal members of the family involved as well as the headmen of the clan sat on mats facing one another and listened or dozed over the long-winded homilies—"here we are present . . ."—and between the periods of discourse a servant would pour out generous portions of intoxicating *octli*. This was more than marriage: clan was involving itself with clan; new blood was being brought into the family holding corporation.

Once the torrents of speech ended—then, in an effort to thwart the supernatural forces that surround this new life-adventure, the man and girl seated on their grass-mat had the knot tied, and they were united.

There was no fixed rule as to whether the man went to live with the woman's clan or if she moved to his. Of a certainty the man did not partake of his bride during the first nights; these rites of the first nights, always referred to in anthropology as *jus primae noctis,* were enjoyed by the uncles, brothers and even father of the bride. This was not regarded as incest but was done to save them both from the "mysterious miasma of marriage"— the males, the "group-friends" of the bride and groom, taking on this "responsibility" in order to spare the newly married any contact with the forces of the supernatural. If one's Italian can encompass the libretto of Mozart's *Marriage of Figaro* this is the underlying theme of the opera: the Count wishes to possess himself of the lord's ancient prerogative of being the first to sleep with the bride.

The Aztec woman had rights, although they were not as far-reaching as the male's. Thus she could own property in her name, go to the council for justice, and if she was cruelly treated she could obtain a divorce. If divorced, she could marry again; if widowed, she could only marry within the clan of the deceased husband. Sterility was the great onus, the one thing a woman feared, for if she bore no children her man could peremptorily divorce her. To a people so involved in wars and death, children were important and necessary.

Then as now woman's power revolved around Venusberg; she controlled mostly by her organism; she was given the privileges which men concede when they are intoxicated by the fumes of desire. Then as now, woman was supposed to

Fig. 20. Life began and ended with the reading of the horoscope. At birth, old men consulted the *tonalamatl*-horoscope for the lucky and unlucky days in a newborn's life.

be chaste; she could be executed for adultery. Woman was not supposed to have extramarital affairs; a man could, however, provided it was with a married woman. If a married woman was involved in multiple coition and became with child she was not so much a problem as an unmarried one.

Woman naturally did not have all the opportunities afforded to man. Nor did she have, as among the Inca, the opportunity, if she was comely, of being brought out of the remotest regions to Cuzco, there to be precipitated into fame as a "*Ñusta*," a Chosen Woman. The Aztec woman had to rise on her own merit or body, and even when influential her moves had to be made obliquely like the bishop's on a chessboard. By mere chance, she might be at some strategic spot at an opportune moment and so become the "tongue" in history, as in the case of Doña Marina, who was first sold into another tribe by her mother, who had remarried and did not want her presence about her new young husband. But in general she had her "place." A woman might escape it as an individual, but she was drawn back to it as a species. And for good reason. The sole aim of the couple in this or in any other society was to free the female from all that was not purely sexual in order that she produce children. "Like generation," wrote Rémy de Gourmont, "mother love is a commandment, a second condition for the perpetuity of life. . . ."

Concubinage existed in Aztec life. This is a strange condition in a semi-welfare state. The Soviets insist that in theirs prostitution could not exist—it does. Theoretically, in so organized a society as the Aztec, prostitution was not supposed to be. Yet the great warriors of the Aztec had their concubines —"many women as mistresses," writes Bernal Díaz, who saw them. As always, the permanence of war brought much change in the traditional mores of the tribe. Armed conflict, as it does everywhere, loosened the ties of home and parental authority. Moral codes, essentially unstable, are at best only a handbook on the ideals of human happiness. "Morality," one writer has said, "will modify itself according to the mobility of the ideal." We have no precise idea how widespread this concubinage really was, but there was a word for it: *auianime,* meaning courtesan.

11. *Calli:* The House

Once married, the couple built their own house. Like all else it was a communal affair. This was as true within Mexico-Tenochtitlán as it was without. The type of house the *macehualli* built depended on where he was and what he was. Finished, it reflected the "eternal man," the peasant-tribesman. Even the greatest Aztec temples and palaces had their origin in the simple native house. The Maya knew this and immortalized such a peasant house as an element in the decoration of the south wing of the "Nunnery Quadrangle" at Uxmal. Dr. Vaillant confirms that "the great cities of the Aztec had their origin in the simple villages of sedentary tribesmen. . . . These were huts with thatched roofs resting

Fig. 21. An Aztec kitchen. At the left, the woman grinds the corn. At the right, the woman shapes the corncake, *tlaxcalli.* In the center is the *cumal,* on which the corncake is baked.

on walls of wattles smeared with mud. . . ."[54] On the mainland, in the temperate zone of Anáhuac Valley, such houses
persist to this day.

Within the "city" in a clan division, this house might be
of adobe, sealed with adobe "cement" and painted. We know
little about it—all has been destroyed. There is nothing left
here as there was at Machu Picchu or Ollantaytambo in Peru,
where one can follow the evolution of the *kancha* type of
native house into the complexity of the Inca palace. In Mexico and in the Maya country there remain only the temples,
pyramids, ceremonial ball-courts; the link of evolution between
peasant house and florid temple has dissolved.

The interior was partitioned between kitchen and sleeping-
living portions. This can be clearly seen in the fragment of
Aztec codice that gave the genealogy of the *tlatoani*, hereditary chiefs of Azcapozalco, with its illustration of a typical
Aztec house compound. At one end the fire and kitchen; not
a fireplace as we understand it, but rocks of uniform height
sunk into the beaten mud floor which merely contained the
wood. There was no chimney, no windows, no fireplace;
the smoke found its own egress through the interstices of the
grass thatch. The fire was banked at night and blown into
life in the morning by the huff and puff of the women.

As the city grew out of the "floating gardens" it had as
many canals as Venice and usually a house of the common
man in the "city" fronted on a canal. The greater number of
houses, wrote Cortés, "were one story only." The materials,
according to the importance of the buildings, "were *tezontli*
[a volcanic stone easily worked, dull red in color] and adobes
that formed the walls plastered with lime, and in the suburbs
and shores of the island [the houses were constructed] of
reeds and straw, appropriate . . . for the lower classes." Many
had gardens in which grew flowers or medicinal herbs. By
the house wall each had its own steam bath or *temascal*.

The corncakes were baked in the kitchen on a flat ceramic
dish (*cumal*); three-legged pots for boiling and a variety of
wooden spoons and other simple instruments for cooking
were about. In the other section of the house there was a
raised platform of earth on which a grass mat (*petatl*) was
spread. The highest chieftain in the land had nothing better.
This surprised even Bernal Díaz, who wrote that they had
"beds of matting, with canopies above and no better bed is
given, however great the chief may be." The floor was stamped
earth; on it a *petatl* or deerskin; windowless, the grass-thatched
roofs were gabled or hipped; there were no doors, only a
cloth hanging in front of the opening kept out the night

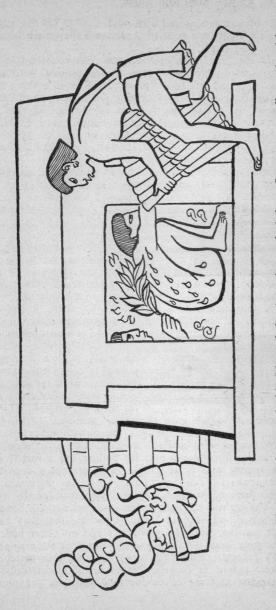

Fig. 22. The *temascal* (steam bath). Most of the Aztec houses had them. Steam was usually produced by throwing water over heated stones.

cold. Clothes hung on pegs driven into walls. Paddles for canoes, weapons, shields with the totemic device of the clan, were usually kept at the temple of the clan, and such personal treasures as the family possessed—jade, feathers, turquoise, festive clothes—were kept in a grass-mat chest, called *petlacalli* (literally "house-chest," a word which for the Aztec was synonymous with "treasure"). There were no tables, few used chairs; there were braziers (see pottery) to keep off the night chill, and for illumination long slivers of pine wood, heavy with pitch, which gave flickering light. Such, with variations depending on rank, were the houses of the common Indian.

The Rhythm of Day and Night

"I must act because I live" were the first words of the homunculus as he issued full-born from the alembic of Dr. Faustus.

Man must live. Before day's break the Aztec throbbed to life with the beat of the wooden-tongued drums from the great temples, as each of the smaller *teocalli* throughout the city took its cue from the largest. As Venus, the morning star, appeared to them at 4 A.M. day was born and the shell trumpets blown by the priests added to the din as all other temples gave counterpoint. Fires that had been banked were blown to life and all over the city of Mexico-Tenochtitlán the pale smoke arose to a windless sky.

The Indian, as farmers do everywhere, rose at this hour before the sun; city or land, the instinct was general. He went to the steam bath, tossed water on the heated rocks, passed through the vapor, dipped into the canal—rich man, poor man, little man, chief, all responded in like manner to the rhythm of Aztec life. Even Moctezuma rose at the same time and went off to the courts to attend the dawn session.

All had morning ablutions. Aztec people were relatively clean since water was available. Over this the Spaniards were unable to hide their surprise, coming from a Europe where it was rare to bathe monthly. Andres de Tapia, a companion of Cortés, affirmed: "Moctezuma bathed twice the day . . . and all [of the Indians] bathed frequently." Since there were no pigs and no fat, the Aztec had no soap as we know it, but he had a natural detergent, the roots of the Saponaria, which the practical-minded Spaniard called the soap-tree (*copalxocotl*); it made a lather and performed the work of soap.

People newly married or too poor to have a slave (*tlacotli*) or too lately wed to have children to help them, had to prepare the corn-mass for the tortillas (*tlaxcalli*) twice daily

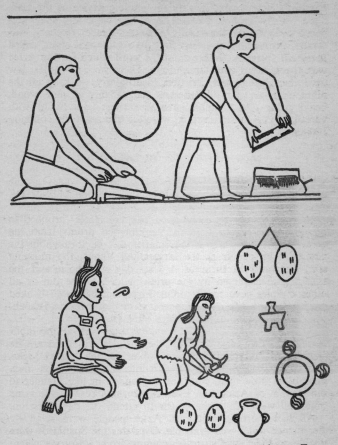

Fig. 23. Independent inventions in the kitchen. Above: Egyptians making bread; from a mural at Thebes dated 1900 B.C. The meal is ground on a stone mortar, and the unleavened bread is baked on a flat oven. The baked bread is illustrated by the two circles. Below: An Aztec girl being instructed by her mother in the art of making corncakes. She grinds on a stone mortar. The circle in front represents the baking device, the *cumal*. On the wall are the baked cakes. From the *Codice Mendocino*.

themselves. There were no short cuts. Dry corn was steeped in lime, then boiled and the corn skin pried loose; then it was brayed on the stone *metate* with a grooved stone roller. This technique of corn preparation is so old that these artifacts appear among the first (as well as the last) archaeological objects to be found in the yielding earth. The unleavened cornbread, pancake-shaped, was baked on a flat *cumal*. This was the non-variable base food of their lives. In addition there were beans, chili pepper, fish, sometimes meat; maize could be made into tamales or *atolli*, a gruel made of maize flavored with honey and chili pepper. The culinary day began and ended with the same food. There were no cattle, goats, pigs, horses, until white men brought them, thus no milk or cheese. There was nothing in all Mexico such as the maté used in Paraguay. Cacao-chocolate was imported from the hotlands and only the well-provided had it. There was no grease for frying—everything was baked or boiled. Food was washed down with the mild *octli* intoxicant; corn was the base of life. All the tribes from Nicaragua to Arizona predicated their lives on it; all the temple-cities reared their economy on it; one's day began and ended with corn, and no matter how exotic were the foods of the Aztec leaders—which so surprised their conquerors—the base remained the simple corncake. No other single plant has played so large a role in the development of cultures.

After this repast in semidarkness, man and woman put food and drink into a basket slung from the neck and went into the fields. If they worked in *chinampas,* these were cultivated; if they had fields assigned to them by the clan on the mainland, they poled their dugout to the fields which they worked alone or collectively with other clan members. However, the high frequency of Aztec conquest and the need to put down rebellions among those newly or anciently conquered made any able-bodied man subject to instant war call. Such was the life of the farmer-warrior.

At night before dusk they were home again and once more there was the business of making corncakes. There were available in the market turkey, duck, deer, beans, squash, *camote,* and such like; the evening meal, the largest, was between four and five. The man or men squatted on the reed mats, helping themselves with their fingers from the pots of food brought to them. Women ate apart.

At night the room was lighted by pine splinters. By this light the women spun or worked their loom or prepared the *pulque* intoxicant; the men made paddles for canoes, grass mats, split their knives, arrowheads, fish needles, from obsid-

ian, or chipped out stone querns; these they would trade in
the market. When children began to make their yearly appearance, they were first placed in a cradle and then as soon
as they could move they became a part of this fabric of life.
Above all—children.

In this state, where war was perpetual and death constant,
a rising birthrate, even though it meant the overpopulation of
the "city" and led in turn to much of the local war, was one
of the important duties of all. As soon as the woman was
pregnant, she was put under the protection of the god Tez-
catlipoca. There is a whole pictured history in the *Codice
Mendocino* of the birth, naming, rearing, discipline, of a child,
of the details of swaddling and the type of cradle.[55] When
the child was born, a magician (*tonalpoulqui*) was brought in
by the parents from their own local clan temple. He consulted
a horoscope (*tonalamatl*), a sort of book of fate, which was
unrolled to its 20-foot length. This was to determine if the
child had been born under good or bad auguries. The naming
was important and if they found that the day was unlucky,
the naming was put off to a better moment—the avoidance
of misfortune itself is the enjoyment of positive good. "What's
in a name?" To the Indians, everything. It is a badge, a
"handle" (in Midwest American colloquial). Many primitives
have two names, social and personal. The personal was known
and used only by the immediate family in the belief that if
used too often, it might lose its power. In times of illness, the
witch doctor used the real name to call the dying back to life.
Boys were called after their fathers or grandfathers, usually
dynamic names, as Smoking Crest (*Chimal-popoca*), Obsidian
Serpent (*Itzcoatl*), Speaking Eagle (*Quauhtlatoa*); girls, who
seem always to evoke a sense of poetry, were named after
flowers, stars, birds, as Ibis (*Atototl*), Green Flower (*Matlal-
xochitl*), or Rain Flower (*Quiauh-xochitl*).[56]

Since there was rank without class, it was not necessary to
remain in a lowly state, even if one were born into it. In Peru
the state existed for the Inca; among the Aztec the state developed for the good of the individual. A man, as Dr. Vaillant
pointed out, "could attain *rank* through his own efforts" [57]
but this rank his children did not automatically inherit "unless
they earned it through equivalent tribal service." This could
be accomplished in various ways—as a good farmer, hunter,
artisan or soldier or even merchant; excelling in any of these
brought leadership.

Schooling of a sort was given at the clan's house for boys
(*telpochcalli*). Each clan maintained a number of these under
the administration of a master (*telpochtlatoque*). In charge

was either a well-known warrior or an elder; here boys learned their own mytho-histories, rituals, and, above all, the use of war weapons. No doubt the master was soon able to ferret out those who showed dexterity with weapons—there was a small cadre of professional soldiers—and the young Aztec might be made to incline in that direction. Artisans and painters were revered too, or the boy might become a merchant, except that there was a tendency for this calling to go direct from father to son; or if he showed mystical leanings, he might be sent to the *calmecac* (which the Spaniards likened to a monastery), there to learn the intricacies of priesthood. In the expanding world of the Aztec much was possible.

On the whole, training of the child remained in the parents' hands. Learning was by mimicry. One can follow the manner of this training in the recorded picture-history. At three years of age, the child is allowed one-half tortilla per day—the tortilla being a foot in diameter; at thirteen he is eating two such outsized tortillas per day. The boy mimics the father; at first he carries a small bag suspended from his neck, for he must be his own dray animal; this is increased monthly until, like his father, he can carry 60 pounds. He fishes, plants, makes dugout canoes; he gathers rushes, weaves *petates*, makes sandals, carries, walks, runs. All of this is recorded in detail with word and picture.

Punishment was not always proportionate to the wrongdoing; certainly Aztec child discipline would not be approved by our overly-timid society, which has created the "progressive child." For some infractions the father held the child's head over smoke; for others he was hand-pricked with a maguey thorn until the blood flowed. Since in these pictures the father is seen talking the while, admonishing while he is punishing (one sees by the speech scroll in front of his face that he is talking) the boy is being trained. This certainly was no worse than the fate Benvenuto Cellini suffered at the age of five when he thought he saw a lizard sitting on the coals of a fire: "My father . . . becoming instantly aware of what the thing was . . . gave me a great box in the ears which caused me to weep and howl with all my might." Cellini was pacified by his father's saying: "My dear little boy, I am not striking you for any wrong . . . but only that you remember that . . . you saw a salamander." [58]

Daughters were like their mothers; dress was identical. At six the young girl is learning to spin; at eight she is sweeping the floors and eating one and a half tortillas per day; at thirteen she is making the tortillas, as she will do twice daily all the rest of her life.

This sense of dedication was the origin of Aztec social behavior. It was based on ancient mores dictated by custom, continued by custom and the authority of the parent. What was done is done; what is not, is not. Above all, their virtue was as the ancient Romans knew the word. The orientation of the Roman mind was as farmer-soldier, and although removed by time and distance, what has been said of Roman virtue in the farmer-soldier could be repeated for the Aztec: "Unremitting work is the lot of the farmer, for the seasons wait for no man . . . accidents of weather and pest may frustrate him; he must accept compromise and be patient . . . routine is the order of his life . . . the life of the fields is his life . . . to him the knowledge born of experience is worth more than speculative theory. His virtues are honesty and thrift, forethought and patience, work and endurance and courage, self-reliance, simplicity and humility in the face of what is greater than himself." [59]

12. The *Milpa*-Fields

Aztec life revolved around the *milpa*—the corn field. And for good reason. No other civilization that has left its footsteps on the road of time has been predicated on the use of a single plant such as Indian corn (*centli*). Earlier than 3000 B.C., the cultures of the Middle East—Assyrian, Sumerian, Egyptian—were cultivating such leguminous plants as pulses, peas, lentils, vetches, whose high protein content made storage easy in semi-desert lands. As for cereals such as wheat, "that most important extra-tropical grain," * it had been cultivated in India since Mesolithic times.⁶⁰ "Wheat . . . barley, rye, millet, panic-grass" were all part of the diet and economy of all who flourished in the "fertile crescent." Yet none of these aforementioned civilizations depended solely on one plant as did those of Mexico and Yucatan.

The Egyptians, to give one pertinent example, according to the Papyrus Harris (Dynasty XX *c*. 1200 B.C.) knew over thirty types of bread—the Aztec had one. Their diet was varied: peas, lentils, watermelons, artichokes, lettuce, endive, radishes, onions, garlic, leeks. They had fats, both vegetable and animal—the Aztec had none. They had beef, honey, dates, as well as milk and cheese and even butter, which was unknown to the Aztec until A.D. 1525. The stomach led in this refusal of man to accept his environment as fixed—"it is from the kitchen" that "so many technical operations" have sprung, e.g., furnaces, ovens, preservation, fermentation, grinding techniques. Independent inventions in the kitchen can be easily discerned by comparing the Egyptian women making unleavened bread, as in the drawings of their baking on the wall at Thebes *c*. 1900 B.C., with the kitchen of the Aztec woman who is preparing unleavened tortillas in A.D. 1520.

Corn made settled life possible in Mexico and elsewhere. Since these people had but one such grain, it is understandable why it played so great a part in ritual and in practice. The

* Emmer, an early wheat, has been found in Troy II (2300 B.C.).

origin of this grain is enveloped in botanical controversy. Although some geneticists believe that the greatest diversity of varieties comes out of Mexico, this is disputed. Paraguay is suggested as the point of dissemination by some, challenged by others. For the moment, "present evidence points to a dissemination in all directions of the early forms from an unknown center." [61] In the beginning of the twentieth century, it was easy to state that maize—(the Awarak-Carib name for corn)—developed out of *teosinte (euchlaena)* which was considered to be the ancestor of corn much as wild grass was the ancestor of wheat. Today the botanical applecart has been upset by findings that point to a hybrid between a species of tripsacum and maize as the origin-corn, (both teosinte and tripsacum will cross with maize); and one of our great geographers who is not easily stampeded into "Asiatic contacts" has stated—to make it still more complex—that the origin of maize "cannot even now be attributed with certainty to the New World as long as certain matters concerning Southeastern Asia remain unsolved." [62] Whatever the distribution centers, well-developed corncobs two inches in length have been found in graves on the desert coast of Peru, radio-

Fig. 24. *Chinampas,* the "floating gardens" agriculture of the Mexican lakes. Into immense reed baskets, the Aztec put earth, then planted trees, anchoring the "floating garden" with staves. Out of these Mexico City grew.

carbon-dated 2500 B.C. Since one must begin at the beginning as Alice did in her Wonderland, we can begin at that date and allow those who wish to follow the maze of maize to pursue it. The starting point is in the bibliography.

Milpa culture has remained unchanged for 3,000 years. What is true of Aztec farming technique is true of all others in this milieu. Milpas were distanced 2 to 15 miles from the dwellings. If the land was forested, trees were ringed a year before and felled with ax-shaped stone celts. The bush and trees being burned, the ash was turned into the soil; larger trees were allowed to rot with time and provide humus. The earth was turned over and prepared by means of a digging stick (*coa*). March was the planting time. Corn kernels were placed in holes 4 to 5 inches deep; in temperate zones beans and squash were put in at the same time; corn, growing faster, acted as host plant for the vines. April brought rain, and if the desired rain was withheld by the gods, sacrifice was made to *Tlaloc*, the rain-god. Of the eighteen months of the Aztec year, almost every one had its ceremonies and dances connected with the growing and harvesting of corn. The corn ripened in July and there was a feast for the Goddess of Young Corn (see under *Religions and Festivals*). In August the rain which had been petitioned in April had to be held back; the Aztec had somehow to cajole the gods not to send rain so as to spoil the harvest. So, another sacrifice; this time to a mature woman representing the Goddess of Ripe Corn.

What did all this yield the Indian in food? The studies made among the Maya can apply approximately to the Aztec, even though Maya agriculture in the hotlands had slightly more yield.[63] An acre gave 20 bushels of husked corn, a bushel being 56 pounds, which, fortuitously, coincides with a "cargo," or what a man could carry on his back. The average size of a milpa in Yucatan was 10 acres; it would have been slightly less in the land-hungry Aztec territory. This gave an Aztec family a yield of 200 bushels of corn yearly, or 11,200 pounds. To fell, plant, weed and harvest this land with the aid of his wife and, say, four half-grown children, the Aztec farmer would have to expend about 200 days. In the same field he would also plant beans, squash, pumpkins, adding to the yield of the field and also to be counted within the produce of these 200 days. Now since the average consumption of corn for tortillas is 1½ pounds a day, the family consumed only one third of what it produced, or 3,276 pounds' consumption as against 11,200 of yield, allowing a surplus for barter, trade, work taxes and religious taxes. With a surplus of 165 unused days unless he was called to battle, the Aztec could use these in his particular craft, making grass mats, fiber sandals, canoes, weapons, etc. These he bartered for needed things at the markets.*

Corn was the "basic." What else? Beans (*etl*) were grown in the same *milpa*, using the cornstalks for support, and squash and pumpkins, all of the genus *cucurbita*, as well as the crooked-necked variety (*ayote*) were planted in between.

The other "basic," the potato, which nourished half of prehistoric South America, the Aztec never had; as a cultivated plant it was unknown throughout Mexico *until it was brought back by the Spanish*. It first was carried to Spain, then it appeared in Europe as an article of diet for the poorer man,

* The problem in this arcadia remained land. Neolithic agricultural methods made constant demand for new land, hence wars to acquire it. As there was little or no crop rotation and only insignificant fertilization, milpas were planted only two years in succession, then allowed to lie fallow for ten years before again beginning the cycle. "Thus," reasoned Dr. Morley in *The Ancient Maya*, "if the average cornfield is 12 acres in size and each field is in corn for only two years, *it will take 72 acres of land to maintain the average family permanently*. That is, to support a village of 500 people (100 families) 7,200 acres or about 11.2 square miles are necessary."

Fig. 25. Aztec corn bins in which the harvested grain was kept. At the left, a woman stores corn grains in a large ceramic urn; at the right, a woman holds the *tamale*, still a popular food after 3,000 years.

being introduced into England by Sir John Hawkins in 1565;
then it returned to America. In Mexico it appeared "as an item
of European diet," and in present-day Mexico, the potato is
grown only for sale to those of a higher social position. However, the potato was nowhere cultivated in Mexico or North
America until after the Conquest. This is curious because wild
tuber-bearing *solanums* are found as far north as Colorado.
When the potato arrived, the Aztec did not even have a name
for it; they called it *pelon-camotli* "the Peruvian sweet potato." *There was never any direct communication between
Peru and Mexico* until white man appeared.[64]

The Aztec had the sweet potato (*camotli*); it grew in the
warmer valleys below 6,000 feet. An *ipomea*, a tuber-bearing
morning glory, it is one of a great family of over 100 species
found throughout the world; many are tuber-bearing. The
Chinese had the yam, which is Old-World in origin; they
called it *shu*. This yam, which is a *discorea*, is found
throughout Polynesia extending down to New Zealand, where
it was assiduously cultivated by the Maori. But one cannot
botanically equate the *camote* with the yam; they are different
plants, though they are constantly confused with one another
in the United States. Few Europeans are acquainted with one
or the other so that when Thor Heyerdahl, the Wrong-Way
Corrigan of anthropology, wrote didactically that "[Kon] Tiki
brought . . . in the fifth century the Peruvian sweet potato to
New Zealand," [65] it is the apogee of botanical ignorance.

The Aztec developed, if not all the plants, then the names
of much which is common on our table today: tomatoes
(*tomatl*) grew below the frost line, planted in dormant milpas;
the biting hot peppers (*chilli*), all varieties of *capsicum*, grew
beside the *tomatl;* the gelatinous weeds valued as food for
infants and the sick; various Amaranth pigweeds, which they
called *huautli*, were cultivated and made into flat cakes. Pine-
apples, which originated in the warmer areas from Panama
to Brazil, reached Mexico probably from the West Indies and
were grown as far north as Jalisco, appearing as high as 6,000
feet altitude. When they could, the Aztec cultivated them.
The very observant Jesuit traveler José de Acosta tasted
them in Mexico in 1565 and found them "very coole, full of
liquor and of easie digestion and in time of heate, fit to
refresh." Cortés sent one to Spain "to our Emperor *Charles*
which must have cost much paine and care to bring it so
far . . . yet he did not trie the taste." [66]

Avocados—the Mexican word *ahuacatl* evolved into *ahua-
cate*, avocado—were grown in the warmer valleys of Aztec
territory. The chewing-gum tree *chicle-zapotl* has come

directly down to us in name and product. Chocolate (*choco-latl*), the beverage and the word, came to us from the Mexican farmer who cultivated the tree when his lands reached the lower warmer areas; it thrived on the Pacific side as far north as Tepic. Everywhere chocolate appeared as an important element in native culture. It was an Aztec passion, sweetened with wild honey, perfumed with vanilla, tinctured with *achiote*. Moctezuma quaffed it from pure gold cups: "a certaine drink from cacao, served with great reverence."

The preparation and working of the milpa cornfield was collective. Members of the clan assisted one another, and when a farmer-warrior was away to the wars, his fields were cultivated by others of his clan. While the number of plants under cultivation seems impressive, agriculture was not as advanced as among the Inca. They did not prepare elaborate terracing as was done in the Andes; they were not soil-makers, except in the expedient of the *chinampas;* they had no fertilizer other than their own feces, where the Inca had bird guano and llama offal; irrigation was casually developed because of the nature of the land; the fall-off of the rain could not be harnessed as was done in Peru. Irrigation techniques, which are inseparable from a developed agriculture, were of a poor order. The Aztec's dependence on rain is the "reason why" for the ceaseless preoccupation with the appeasement of the gods and with conquests, the wars for more tribute and for more sacrificial victims in order to cajole the rain-god into proffering the withheld gifts of rain. As the good will of the rain-god could only be sustained by a diet of human hearts, and as these could only be provided by taking prisoners in battle, a long peace was a disaster. Only in perpetual war was there safety.

It was a nightmare.

13. Tax Contributions to the State

Everything, even in such a moneyless society as the Aztec, had, unfortunately, to be paid for; taxes and death to the common Aztec *macehaulli* were as inevitable as conception. Babylon invented money, this symbol that made life simplified all over the world. But because of geographic isolation, no civilization in prehistoric America knew money, if one excepts the use of cacao-money. "The Cacao is a fruit little lesse than almonds," José de Acosta tells us. "They use it in steede of money for with five cacaos they buy one thing, with thirtie another and with a hundred another, without any contradiction . . . from it theye make a drincke which they call Chocolate."

Taxes, whatever the reality of cacao-money, were paid in work-service and seem to have been assessed through the clan. "The tribal council divided the land among the clans and the leaders of each in turn apportioned its share among the heads of families justly and equitably." [67] Sections were also reserved for the maintenance of the chief of the temple staff, for war supplies and the payment of tribute. Other portions of this land controlled directly by the clan were worked communally and the yield—whether corn, beans or agave fibers—was paid as tribute-tax to the central tribal council for the maintenance of religion, war, the "king" and his various non-taxpaying staff, (priests, army, craftsmen, concubines, keepers of the royal aviary), and for the engineering works in and beyond Mexico-Tenochtitlán and all the other paraphernalia of state with which we today are so fully familiar.

In addition to the foodstuffs which were sent to the central granaries and noted down in the account books by the Tribute-Recorder of the "Chief Speaker," the clan group was also called upon for levies of man power to build public buildings. Under direction from architect-builders, who were tax-exempt, dikes, aqueducts, roads, were built. The "king" of the Aztec also had lands which were cultivated by clans in rotation, and the usufruct of this also went into the official deposits.

"Tell me what you eat: I will tell you what you are," wrote Jean Anthelme Brillat-Savarin in his *Physiologie du Goût*,[68] written in Connecticut while he waited for the French revolution to burn itself out. This aphorism could apply to all Neolithic theocracies, especially the Aztec. Frequent comparisons have been made between the temple-cities in America and those in Sumer. In primitive societies all were farmers, for "in a hypothetical pure Neolithic economy there would be no full-time specialist." When farming improved a surplus was produced and granaries were attached to the temples, in Sumer as in America. As man became completely dependent on agriculture and as sun and rain were derived from the gods, who "owned" the soil they tilled, the first fruit "tithes" (in Christian parlance) were given to the temple to support the galaxy of priests who acted as the intermediaries for the gods. These surpluses were used to aggrandize the temple, secure the interest of the priestly class, and provide exchange for the import of raw materials they lacked. The administration of all this produced the temple-city, and so there came into being the specialists: craftsmen, administrators, clerks *(tlacuilo-*writers in Mexico), who put down receipts and expenditures. These early temple accounts are among the oldest cuneiform writing in Sumer (3500 B.C.), and their Aztec counterparts constituted, until they were destroyed, some of the oldest Aztec records.

It is obvious that the directing class themselves did not personally consume all that poured into Mexico-Tenochtitlán; this was used to compensate the specialists. The surplus was also stored for general use during crop failures. Since accounts had to be kept, some archaeologists believe this was one of the factors which brought about the invention of writing.*

That the Inca, which was also a tribute-state, should have developed only the *quipu* and not writing, remains one of the earth-mysteries.

* V. Gordon Childe writes that the "standardization of conventional graphic system" stimulated the invention of writing. "The art of reading and writing [he is writing about the lands of Mesopotamia] became an accomplishment with considerable prestige. The initiates were exempted from all manual tasks." Further, they were trusted with the task of thinking for the society. This was duplicated in Aztec society.

14. The Loom: A Woman's Art

Weaving was one thing that belonged wholly to woman. She gathered the fiber, prepared it, spun, dyed, and then loomed it; no male intervened. It is a fact sometimes overlooked that, in this strange world where everyone was a craftsman in one form or another, the anonymous and communal weaving artisans were all women. Theirs was also an ephemeral art. None of the millions of pieces loomed has survived and all we know of Aztec design is that which has come down to us in the Book of Tributes or else those painted on pottery and on murals.

The Aztec back-strap loom was simple. The type is known, with little variation, throughout all the Americas. Two wooden rods are fastened, one to each end of the warp, to

Fig. 26. Weaving was the woman's art. At the left, she uses the typical back-strap loom; to the right, carded cotton is put into thread on a spindle-whorl which rests in a ceramic bowl.

stretch the cloth to desired length; the lower one is attached to the back of the weaver (hence the name "back-strap"), while the upper is tied to a post or tree. Three feet wide, the warp was loomed by means of a shuttle woven between the strands of the stretched yarn: that simple. And yet from these looms came, if one can trust the hyperbole of the conquistador, some of the finest weavings they had ever seen. "Eight damsels, they were," wrote Bernal Díaz, "all eight of them clothed in the rich garments of the country, beautifully ornamented. . . ."

The Aztec when they were "wanderers" used the fiber of the maguey *(metl)*, a spined succulent which, after corn, was one of Mexico's most beneficent plants. It provided them with intoxicating drink *(octli);* rope fiber, which, under the name "henequen," is a well-known commercial product; and numerous other products too many and too varied to be given here. Agave was a primary source of fiber. The pad (technically it is not a leaf) of this succulent is veined with strong fibers, which, when dried, combed, and spun, can be made sufficiently delicate to spin; from this fiber of the maguey *ixtle,* a very coarse linenlike thread, the Aztec women made their first weavings. Later, when they rose in social scale and could barter, they obtained cotton from the warmer valleys. Cotton soon passed from a luxury to a necessity, and one of the principal errands of their traders, who went to the south hotlands for goods or tribute, was to obtain "the indispensable cotton." Women bartered for cotton in the market, or, when it arrived as tribute, it was distributed equally to the clans and each woman weaver obtained her share.

Cotton fibers were spun on the traditional spindle whorl, a slender wooden stick 10 to 12 inches in length, balanced at the lower end by a pottery ring. This is "traditional" in that wherever there has been spinning and weaving the technique of fiber preparation has anciently been the same everywhere. Only a well-versed archaeologist could differentiate between the spindle rings of Palestine (3000 B.C.); Troy (2500 B.C.); Peru (2000 B.C.); Maya (200 B.C.) or Aztec (A.D. 1300). Curiously enough, all that is left of the greatest art of Mexico and Yucatan is the ceramic spindle whorl. All else—weavings, loom, even the sticks—has succumbed to time. The method of spinning the fiber, the "business end" left in a small ceramic bowl, has been pictured by the Aztec themselves.

The fibers after spinning were dyed, with urine as mordant to "fix" the color. Dyes were mostly vegetable: *achiotl* (the Bixa species) yielded red—this, under the name of *anatto,* was later used in our own economy to dye oleomargarine; anil, a shrub, gave a dark blue; cochineal, a scale insect parasite was, as its Latin name *coccus cacti* implies, gathered on the cactus by Indians, who obtained from it a carmine color; and there were others. The dark seed of the genipa, found on a tree in the hotlands, gave off a black color; a lavender color came, like the "royal purple of Tyre," from a mollusk found along the Pacific coast.

Color was more than color. It was symbolism, and, to the Aztec, very real. If red was used as blood, it became the actual equivalent of blood; it *was* blood. Black represented war because black obsidian glass was the cutting edge of battle swords (*maquahuitl*); it was also the symbol of religion: the priests dressed exclusively in it. Yellow was food because it was the color of corn; blue meant sacrifice; and green was royal, because it was the color of the quetzal plumes used only for chieftains. The French symbolists led by Mallarmé at the end of the nineteenth century used color in the same way in their poetry, and when they assailed all Paris with the allegories and esotericism of these ancient theurgies what they believed to be so new was in reality as old as the world itself.

Design had no horizons—everything was allowed, everything permitted. Protected by the goddess *Xochiquetzal*, the weaver expressed anything that she felt. Of nature and realism, there were the things of the earth—sun, fish, snails, cactus, bird feathers, tiger skins, even falling snow, were used as motifs; there were geometric designs, highly stylized animals, transformation of representational art into all-over patterns. All this is suggested in the designs taken from the Book of Tributes and redrawn from the actual weavings delivered to Mexico-Tenochtitlán.

For themselves women wove the skirts ankle length, elaborately bordered, and for the top part of the costume the well-known *huipilli*. Their art sense ran riot. The striking effect of the women's dress was not overpainted by the conquistador. Consider this description by a padre during the festivals of the month when the women, especially the beautifully dressed concubines, danced with the soldiers: ". . . and all were well-clothed, beautifully adorned, all had wonderfully wrought skirts and pretty *huipilli*. The skirts were decorated with designs representing hearts, others a fish motif, others with spirals or leaves, some were of a simple weave; they all had frames, hems and fringes. . . . As to the blouses, some had loose dark adornments, others motifs representing smoke or black stripes and some with houses or fishes. . . ."[69]

For the men, women wove two principal garments: the

breechclout *(maxtlatl)*, a single piece with highly decorated ends which went about the waist, and a long cloak *(tilmantli)*, which knotted at the shoulder, since they had neither brooches, pins nor buttons. A portrait of Nezahualpilli, "king" of Texcoco and allied with Tenochtitlán, shows such a costume elaborated for so exalted a person.

War kept the women further occupied. They wove a coarse cloth of cotton for the war dress *(xicolli)*, and also as a protection against arrows, a quilted cotton jacket not unlike that which the Chinese use against the cold. These the Spaniards thought superior to their own steel armor.

The priests wore ankle-length black ponchos and got them from the looms of young virgins assigned to the temples. As befitting the necromancy of their beliefs, they were bordered with skull and crossbones.

15. Pottery and Pottery Makers

Pottery, like weaving and house building, was part of the Aztec cultural equipment. All made pottery in one form or another even if all did not make *fine* pottery. This self-sufficiency is what prompted Aldous Huxley in his Mexican travels to extoll "the primitives' human wholeness." [70] Pottery making confirms the point that "a primitive is forced to be whole—a complete man, trained in all the skills of the community . . . if he is not whole, he perishes." All of the tribes were pottery makers, those of Cholula being especially famed for their red and black ware. It was mostly a craft industry done at home with the leisure time allowed from agriculture. A number of pottery makers who rose in public esteem as artisans left agriculture entirely and organized the guild of pottery makers. Utilitarian pottery, coarse-grained and designed for heavy duty, was used for cooking. Three-legged pots, the large *cumal* which was a flat disk-shaped griddle for baking tortillas, bowls with roughened surface to act as graters for braying *chilli*-peppers—these, with pottery goblets for *pulque*, were part of every household. The finer pieces of delicate pottery almost as thin as good china, the beautifully decorated kind the archaeologists find in graves, were for the dead.

There was more to pottery than mere pots and drinking bowls. Spindle whorls, which weighted the spinning distaff like a flywheel, and spinning sticks too, were made of clay. Ceramic dolls were made with jointed arms. Toys were made with wheels, although the idea of putting the wheel to any other use never occurred to them. The little clay gods, gods of fertility and corn, were mass produced in clay forms; the cult "figurine" was dropped by the farmer into his cornfield to conjure the good will of the local genii for a better corn crop. Each household had its charcoal brazier to snuff out the chill, and temples had large ceramic braziers the height of a man, coalescing beauty and utility, a "ritualistic usefulness with architectural ornament"; there were clay stamps and seals used for stamping cloth and *amatl*-paper, a step in the evolution of printing. After ideographic writing, the next inevitable step (as the Chinese saw it) was to reduce the ideograph to a symbol and "print"—impress the seal on paper. Thus with these pottery stamps and *amatl*-paper they were very close to true printing.

Pottery, apart from its beauty of form is an important record to the archaeologist. Potsherds may be dismal to read about and equally dismal to work over but they represent a type of history. A preliterate people give more precise information in their pottery than in their legends and architecture. Much can be determined from the stylistic changes effected in pottery. A new god-cult arrives, a new epoch is ushered in, a new age—it is first reflected in pottery. A conqueror comes, and the temples remain standing, but the common people echo the change—we have seen the same thing in our late wars—reflecting the conqueror in style of clothes, manners, habits; pottery is a guided sequence to advance and decline. By using potsherds to establish spatial

Fig. 27. Aztec ceramics. These are the types that were made for use and export at the height of Aztec power. The long-handled ceramic was used by priests in the burning of *copal* to remove the disease of newness. The other vessels were for eating and drinking.

relationships the archaeologist uses some of the techniques of geology: a stratigraphical cut at the kitchen midden of an archaeological site reveals the debris of the process of living. Pottery products are mixed with all the other artifacts and are imperishable. In painting, design, materials, techniques, they reveal age and establish a relative chronology.

Pottery was functional in this society of craftsmen. It brought psychological fulfillment—handcrafts are one of the therapeutic techniques of the psychiatrist; it had social utility—an economy based upon handcraft culture is not so liable to fluctuations as one based on mass-produced products. Naturally, the Aztec, who knew nothing of such reasoning, thought only of using the surplus pottery production as an exchange medium at the weekly market.

Fig. 28. Various other pottery forms used in Aztec households. These were all utilitarian and were not placed in graves or tombs.

16. The *Tiaquiz*-Market

The market is like Napoleon's measure of Switzerland; if such a state did not exist it would have to be invented—an uninvolved ground in which warring nations trade. The idea that trade is sacrosanct is as old as society itself; the market did not have to be "invented"; it came into being wherever man lived and traded, sold and bartered. Yet even so the Mexican market was astonishing. . . .

"When we arrived at the great market place," remembered the chronicler,[71] "we were astounded at the number of people . . . and the quantity of merchandise and the good order and control that was maintained." "Yes," agreed Hernán Cortés after visiting the same market "there are daily more than sixty thousand people bartering and selling . . . the square is twice as big as Salamanca . . . every kind of merchandise . . . is for sale. . . . There is a street of game [partridges, turkeys, quail, pigeons, parrots, owls, kestrels]. . . . There is a street of herb sellers . . . roots and . . . medicinal herbs . . . and houses of the apothecaries in which they sell the medicines from these herbs. . . . There are barber shops where you may have your hair washed and cut."[72] And as if they vied with each other, Bernal Díaz recalled "other wares," i.e., "Indian slaves [*tlacotli*] both men and women . . . brought in as the Portuguese bring Negroes from Guinea . . . tied to long poles." Next there were "traders . . . who sold great pieces of cotton . . . and articles of twisted thread." Much in evidence was the coarse cloth spun from the fibers of the maguey and used by those who carried cargo on their backs, and the sandals made of the same fiber. Cortés wrote of the various animal skins for sale and the pottery "of very good quality"; and his companion asked that they not forget the "paper" offered for sale . . . which in this country is called *amatl*, and reeds scented with liquid amber . . . and tobacco and the dyes from cochineal . . . and I am forgetting those who sell salt and those who make the stone-knives." There were "dealers in gold and silver [this would have been impossible in Peru where the Inca 'owned' all metals] and precious stones, feathers and feather mantles." And along with all this commercial activity, there was order. "A very fine building." Cortés assured his liege, Carlos V, "stands in the great square and serves as a kind of audience where ten or twelve persons are always seated, as judges, who deliberate on all cases arising in the market and pass instant sentences on wrongdoers."

Such was the *tiaquiz*-market, of which there were five on the island. Every city on the mainland had its own *tiaquiz* and the festive days were so arranged that the people could attend the various ones within the circuit of the valley of Anáhuac.

While the Mexican market was large, perhaps the greatest, it was not unique: the market at Cholula was a mecca because of its great temple to Quetzalcoatl, which drew people from all over Mexico. Even those who were traditional enemies held their enmities in abeyance while they carried on trade. Trade was sacred. The Spaniards who, on their march to Mexico entered Tlascala, a tribal state in perpetual war with the Aztec, found a city which Cortés thought "larger than Granada . . . with a market in which more than 30,000 people daily are occupied in buying and selling . . . nothing

Fig. 29. Activity at the *tiaquiz* (market). To the left, a woman offers, but a man refuses to trade. To the right, a sale is made by a salt seller.

is lacking. There are gold, silver and precious stones and jewellers' 'shops' . . . there is earthen-ware . . . as fine as any in Spain . . . there are booths for washing your hair and barbers to shave you . . . there are also public baths . . . and good order for . . . they behave like a people of sense and reason . . . the foremost city of Africa cannot rival them."

If march meant markets, men marched. It is incredible, until one sifts the evidence, the distances men walked from the earliest times to market surplus and buy up their lack. Long before 2500 B.C., man in many parts of the world was going to the markets. "The extreme parts of the inhabitable world," wrote the Greek geographer Herodotus, who visited many of them himself, "possess the most excellent products." All of the early routes were luxury routes and the markets were luxury markets. Persia's roads were crowded "with men on the king's business"; people were drawn to trade in the remote Indus Valley so early that when Alexander the Great ventured into it expecting something else "he found well-made roads built of clay-brick" and all manner of "trees bearing yellow fruits lining the way." Whether it was early China trade or the Danube traffic or the "fertile crescent" which drew man, all were bent on ridding themselves of surplus and gaining luxuries. Trade was the loadstone that drew man to its world markets.

The Aztec market, which included tribute in its wares, differed little in the beginning from the usual "American" system of war tribute. But the Aztec systematized it, and every six months 371 vassal cities yielded tribute of products so varied and vast that elaborate account books were needed to keep track of it. The market was further fed by the activities of its wandering merchants. Bernal Díaz himself said: "But why do I waste so many words in recounting what they sell in that great market?—for I shall never finish if I tell all in detail. . . ."

17. The Festival Days

The festival was almost continuous in ancient Mexico.

It is not easy to separate festive and ceremonial, sacred and secular, since everything was bound up together. It is not difficult, however, to find a parallel in times not far distant when hangings and garrotings were always an occasion for holidays, and to realize how, in affairs of this kind, festival and sacred ritual were interlocked.

Like all other advanced tribes the Aztec had a solar calendar, divided into eighteen 20-day months; every one of these eighteen months had ceremonies and festivals. Months had descriptive names. The 1st month was Atlcoulaco ("want of water") and there were ceremonies, parades and sacrifice. The 2nd month was Tlacaxipeualiztli (the "boning of the men"), which for sixteen days had ceremonies and parades when priests danced in the flayed skins of sacrificial victims. This skin, naturally, had magic powers—it gave to the priest who danced in it the power of the undead (i.e., the sacrificial victim whose skin it was); nor was this skin merely a symbol, something that prefigures, as a symbol is to us—it was consubstantiality. We can grasp some of the meaning of this, perhaps, in the story told of an eighteenth-century burgher of Séez who was robbed of some doubloons by his servant. Knowing his rights, after she was tried and executed he exacted the skin of the thief and from it made pantaloons, and whenever the thought of his loss overcame him, he would smack his thigh and cry "The hussy. The hussy."

The 3rd month, Tozoztontli, began with "fasting," and if this did not touch the heart of the rain-god Tlaloc another festival, the flayed-skin dance to Xipé, was performed by the priests. The 4th month brought the people into the city from the fields to celebrate the worship of the new corn; altars in their houses were festooned with cornstalks. It was bloodless this time and young girls gave virginal blessings to the seed corn. By the 5th month (May 3–22) rain was full upon them;

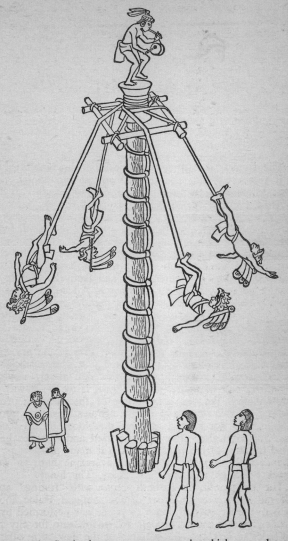

Fig. 30. The flywheel, a game-ceremony in which men, dressed as birds, hung from ropes and rotated, giving the effect of flight. This is still performed in some parts of Mexico.

there were god-impersonation ceremonies, and to make it all very understandable they sacrificed children to the rain-god to thank him (they had sacrificed children in the 3rd month to bring on the rain). It is of course pure calumny to say that anthropophagy was involved in this, although Bernal Díaz wrote: "I have heard it said that they were wont to cook for Moctezuma the flesh of young boys." [73] If that occurred at all, it was a ceremonial cannibalism.

The 7th month (June 12–July 1) was marked with the mimic dances of the salt-workers, who leeched salt from the lakes of Anáhuac. The 8th month (July 2–21) was a joyous one—the adoration of the eating of the corn, an eight-day feast which could not get under way until the priests had despatched a slave girl, beautifully attired to impersonate the Goddess of Young Corn. The 9th month, Tlaxochimaco ("birth-of-flowers"), brought feasts which lasted some days and was unusual in that the two sexes danced together, "even touching the women," as an old Aztec explained. It was the rising class of merchant prince (*pochteca*) that gave the feasts, appropriately, for at the end it was to their god, Yacatecuhtli, protector of merchants.

The 10th month (August 11–30) was ostensibly to celebrate the "fall of the fruits." The people poured in in a festive mood, much as they once did in Europe to see someone drawn and quartered or, even better, beheaded. One has only to see the mischievous drawings of Jacques Callot of the people of Paris rollicking during an execution to see the intermingling of holiday and bloodletting. In the Aztec world the rites to the fire-god Huehueteotl were also certain to attract holiday crowds. Prisoners of war danced together with their captors and then, according to Dr. Vaillant, ascended to the top of a platform where *yauhtli* powder, an analgesic, was blown on their faces to anaesthetize them somewhat during the next minutes. The half-awake prisoners were whirled about a dazzling fire and then dumped into the coals, fished out while still alive to have their still palpitating hearts cut out to be offered to the gods. There followed, after eating and libations of intoxicating *octli*, a competitive climbing of a pole 15 meters high to retrieve various paper insignia on top of it.

The 11th month, from the end of August until September 19, was Ochpaniztli (the "month of brooms"), with, of course, the usual sacrifices. It was also a military month with a review of all the clans parading with new arms and their own insignia on their shields; there was a procession of the knights of the Eagle and the knights of the Tiger (who wore this battle-dress), a phalanx of warriors with special privileges; the festival ended in a gladiatorial contest. The 12th month, Teotleco, marked the return of the gods to earth (*teo,* "god," *tleco,* "return") and good fun for young and old, for ceremonial drunkenness was the rule of the day.

The 13th (September 20–October 9) had to do with Tlacoc, the demanding rain god; the 14th involved a general penance for four days; men were expected to abstain, with ceremony or without it, from their wives. Panquetzaliztli ("feast of the flags"), which was celebrated as the 15th month, honored the war-god first with mock battles; then, says Sahagun, "the women sang and danced . . . intermingling with the men. . . ." They poured jugs of water over their heads—much as was done in the carnivals in Lima—took off their wet clothes, dyed their arms and legs blue, and dressed in *amatl*-paper. The people marked for sacrifice also dressed in paper. It was raining again by the 16th month (December 9–28), and the month's name, Atemoztli, meant "full of waters." The people prepared themselves by fasting five days previous to this feast. They spent the entire night cutting *amatl*-paper "in diverse shapes, stuck them on poles, put them up in their homes and

Fig. 31. Jugglers and musicians enlivened the festive days. Jesters and "Merry Andrews" were part of the equipment of a high-placed Aztec.

invited the symbol of the image they had cut to come together." They made vows, said Sahagun, "and at the same
time took to their drums, their jingles and their tortoise-shell
to play on." The 17th month brought the cold—it was the
end of December. Now they tried to touch the rain-god's
heart, to persuade him to give them the withheld gift of rain.
First the women wept, then the men; the men pelted their
women with straw-filled bags to hurry on the tears. The 18th,
the last month of the year, was to Izcalli. It was a time of
mass sacrifice. The women who were to be immolated were
dressed in *amatl*-paper clothing. After that they repaired to
Cuauhtitlan, where prisoners of war were lashed to scaffolds,
after the manner of the Pawnees of the western plains, and
killed with arrows.

In all, the eighteen Aztec 20-month days totaled 360 days.
The imagination could not encompass more. It was satiated.
There followed the *nemontemi,* "the five empty days" (Febru-
ary 7–11). One did nothing . . . no fire, no music, no love . . .
one sat huddled waiting, waiting. . . .

To picture the life of the Aztec as one long joyous idyl ca-
denced by the beat of the drum to the frenzied dance of
priests would, as one sees here, be wide of the mark. The
Aztec was terrorized as much by life as by the elements. The
phenomenon of a snowstorm—understandably at 7,400 feet
altitude—caused them to search their souls for portents; an
involuntary loss of blood was disastrous; any contact with
woman's catamenial flux would set off a concatenation of
disasters.

Tenochtitlán may have been a paradise, but it was a troubled one.

18. Music

Aztec music—indeed all of "American" music—was tied up with dancing; any "pure" music has disappeared. What remains suggests that Aztec music was strong in rhythm but lacking in tone. This, at least, is what one infers from the instruments: the large upright drum, skin stretched over wood frame *(huehuetl),* was beaten with the bare hands and some control was exercised on the beat and quality of the tone; a smaller counterpart was hung from around the neck and beaten with both hands, but contact with the body spoiled the resonance; the two-noted wooden drum *(teponzatli)* was

Fig. 32. Music and musical instruments. Trumpet, drum, and gourd-rattles gave out the principal effect. The Aztec at the left blows a conch horn. The next man beats a *huehuetl,* an upright drum of stretched skin. Another beats a two-noted wooden *teponzatli*-drum (the beaters were of rubber). The dancing figure shakes the gourd-rattles.

99

beaten with rubber-tipped beaters, sonorous but monotonous. The conch shell—all peoples who have had contact with the sea have had the conch, including the Inca; its use seems to have been world-wide—gave out an impressively deep blast: a chorus of them were used every morning from 4 A.M. to the rising of Venus to arouse the people out of sleep. Since they had no string instruments nor such instruments as the marimba—these were cultural borrowings from Negro slaves —their forte was the percussion instrument in various forms. They also had flutes shaped like pan-pipes, in clay or of reed, and whistles, in addition to the rattles, seed-filled gourds, and the seed or shell attachments on the ankles that kept the beat. These are still used by the present-day Yaqui people. There were also notched bones, usually human femurs, which, rasped with a stick, suggest modern "musica Cubana." The thing to note was that the music was rhythmic, not sonorous; its outward effect was cadence to the dancer, its inward effect, hypnotic.

Dance was as inseparable from music as is singing or rhythmic stress. There were mass dances of various forms and of a certainty there were group dances. But, warriors or priests, merchants or chiefs—under whatever guise, the dance had but one function: to obtain aid from the unseen powers upon which Aztec prosperity depended. Drunkenness itself was ritual and sacred. The dance with music was to seduce the gods; the fundamental, the *raison d'être*, of the dance, to the dancers as well as the watchers, was "mystic communion," [74] the fusion which makes them one with the god they hope will hear their call. Drumming was of supreme importance: it soothed the soul and made the gods amenable. Drumming also exerted a real mystical influence; it acted upon the disposition of the unseen as it acted upon the spectator, so that from the "mystic point of view the drum was an indispensable part of the magico-propitiatory apparatus."

Drum and song were acclaimed together. The singer *(cuicani)* recited his piece:

> Jades I perforate, gold I cast in the crucible;
>   this is my song!
> Emeralds I set . . .
>   this is my song!

Or, with the beat of the bass drum and the two-noted wooden drums giving the added dignity of background, the singer gave out this to the national Aztec god:

I am Hummingbird Wizard, the warrior, no one
   is equal to myself.

Not in vain have I donned my robe of yellow feathers;
   for me the sun has arisen.

Song, music, rhythm, in addition to breaking the dull
monotony of their lives, were used, as they always have been,
for memory. There was little doubt of the effect sought after
by the Aztec impresario. The various episodes of the dance,
the same movements repeated without number, the volumes
of sound, the ornaments and masks, had all one aim, one
religious aim—emotional paroxysms in which all present were
robbed of their self-possesssion and so believed that their wish
to secure the favor of the gods had been attained.

19. Games

Games have always been immense fun. But to the Aztec the "game" was not enough in itself. As with the present-day Russians, it was for them serious business, magical and ritualistic; it had no point of rest. They were more earnest in what was supposed to be unserious than in serious matters. This finds a counterpart in the pages of *La Rôtisserie de la reine Pédauque,* where, in a highly amusing card-playing scene, it is reflected that "men are more punctilious at play than in serious matters and they bring more honesty to bear on tric-trac where it is a passable hindrance and leave it out in battles or in treaties of peace where it would be troublesome." [75]

The passions which man displays in games were best seen in a game played from Honduras to Arizona known as *tlachtli.* It began as a sport; it ended up as ritual. No one can say precisely where or when it began, except that the Olmec who lived in the hotlands of the Gulf Coast, where rubber * grew, had the game as early as 500 B.C.—a ball court was found in their temple-complex at La Venta—and their name was derived from the word for rubber, *olli (Ol-mec:* "the rubber-people").

Tlachtli was already formalized then. Yet the expressive clay figures of tribesmen playing a variant of the game shows it was as popular and ritualistic as American baseball—if one must have an analogy. It was played in a court shaped like a double "I"; walls of tiered seats were on either side; in the middle of this was the "basket," a stone or wooden ring set, not horizontally as in basketball, but vertically; the object was to put the rubber ball through the ring. The ball was

* Charles Marie de la Condamine (1701–74) was the first to experiment with rubber. He found it in use as a sort of syringe by Indians in the Amazon. Rubber from Vera Cruz was first mentioned by Oviedo, the Spanish historiographer, in 1500.

hard, not inflated; the players were allowed to strike it only with legs or hips or elbows; they were padded as is a goalie in ice-hockey. Although many may have played it, yet *tlachtli* was a religious game performed before the rulers of tribes, wherever they were. In Mexico-Tenochtitlán, the ball court stood in the sacred enclosure in front of the racks of skulls of those who had been sacrificed at the main temple, and was bounded on one side by the temple dedicated to the knights of the Eagle.

In other games also the Aztec were certainly as "punctilious in play as in serious matters." *Patolli*, something like back-gammon or parchesi, was a less sanguine sport and was played on a marked board or paper, with beans for counters. The obect was to travel about the board and return "home" to win. It is doubtless the same game that Cortés used to play with Moctezuma when he was the Spaniards' captive in his own palace. Bernal Díaz called it *totoloque*. It was a gam-bling game, as he said, played "with some very smooth pellets made of gold. . . . They toss these pellets some distance as well as some little slabs which were also made of gold. . . . In

Fig. 33. *Tlachtli* was the first basketball game. Popular as well as ritualistic, it was played in a rectangular court with stone "baskets" placed vertically. The ball was of hard rubber. The game was known and played from Honduras to Arizona.

five strokes or tries they gained or lost certain pieces of gold or rich jewels that they staked." *

There were others, mostly played by children, that have their counterparts in our own life. But all this was the plaything of the little man before ritual and the gloomy pessimism of Aztec life turned his naturally gay exuberance into something lugubrious.

* There were only two players but each had his own official scorekeeper. Cortés had Pedro de Alvarado (called "the Sun" by the Aztec because of his white-blond hair), and Moctezuma observed that Alvarado always marked more points than Cortés gained and "courteously and laughingly he said he was being done ill because Cortés was making so much *yxoxol* in the game," i.e., he was "cheating."

Fig. 34. *Patolli,* a game utilizing a board shaped like a cross, was played something like parchesi. Although a game of chance, and used for gambling, *patolli* was semi-sacred and was watched over by the Macuil-xochitl, the Five-flower goddess.

20. The Expediency of Justice

"Codes of law," said Rabelais when he stopped pantagruel-izing long enough to be very serious, "are founded upon necessity and not upon justice." And the Aztec would have agreed. They were not versed in the dialects of "as if"; their justice was exacting, swift, final. What was crime? Stealing, adultery, blasphemy, killing and drunkenness (unless it was ritual). All these were capital crimes. It is difficult to under-stand that a nation given to such an overwhelming sacrificial slaughter would be so aghast at death. But there was a funda-mental difference: war and ceremonial sacrifice, murder and rape during battle, did not involve the clan or tribe. This does not differ in practice from our own moral phenomena—"there is no such thing as moral phenomena, only a moral interpretation of phenomena"; we reward the killer during war and consider murder beyond the pale during peace.

Aztec society, as do all societies, existed (in theory and mostly in practice) for the benefit of its component parts. Their ideas of justice were ancient. Stealing to them was an aberration, for which restitution in kind was the usual pen-ance. For things that could not be restored, there was death or else expulsion from the clan (the same thing), or into slavery. Adultery brought death, although this varied much with the circumstances of the people involved. Punishment to tribesmen who misused the "king's way," the Aztec road, was severe. Robbery of merchants carrying on "sacred business" was death by stoning—commerce and the royal way were sacrosanct. The prognosis for murder naturally was death.

The most heinous were religious crimes. The robbing of temples, an offense that might provoke the disfavor of the gods, or doubting the efficacy of prayers, in short to blaspheme (to blame) anything that might bring disaster on the whole tribe —this brought immediate death. It was no different in the Christian world; an auto-da-fé reported from Seville in the *Fugger News Letters* in 1579: [76] "sentence the *third* Juan de Color, slave, 35, reviled the name of Our Dear Lady and other saints—disputed her miracles . . . burning at the stake."

105

Witchcraft was the deadliest of crimes. Obsession with it is interwoven in the deepest fibers of the primitive mind, especially if it was directed towards someone of one's own clan. It was the worst crime that one could commit, and to cause death by witchcraft was considered worse than murder —it was anthropophagy, i.e., the eating of one's own kin's flesh. The sentence of death was done only after long-drawn-out torture. To remain impartial, however, we must recall the prevalence of witches in our own world. There was the notorious witch Walpurga Hausmann, who, as reported in one of the *Fugger News Letters,* confessed in 1587 to killing forty-three children over a period of thirty years. The bishop of Augsburg gave the verdict: "despatch from life by burning. . . ." And on another tried for misdeeds of witchcraft who, "as the result of her fervent petitioning her sentence has been lightened . . . first she will be strangled and only then burned."

The administration of justice was designed so that people would live in harmony among themselves. (It was not designed for their neighbors, for all men are enemies.) They lived by a code far more strict than the one we impose on ourselves. In the eternal theater of carnage and death that was Aztec, one had to conform. . . .

Fig. 35. Aztec justice as shown in the *Codice Florentino* and drawn by an Aztec artist. Three chieftains condemn a criminal for an outrageous crime, and witness his execution, by garroting.

21. Medicinal Plants

Medicinal plants in the Aztec world were of a wide and interesting order. Few protohistoric peoples have left so extensive a description of plants, economic, aesthetic and curative. The Aztec, like all other "Mexicans" before them, were metaphysicians far more spontaneous than we ourselves. They wore amulets to protect against disease—an arm stricture, a nose ornament, a lucky shell or stone, a talisman to avert a baleful influence. Diseases, numbered among the disasters, were caused by unseen powers: defense was made by appealing to the same medium. Although not completely unaware of the pathological, their medicine was bound up with magic and religion. Yet since life is a lying dream and physics ofttimes

Fig. 36. The cure-doctor *(ticitl)* at work. An old woman, as shown in the *Codice Florentino,* applies leaves to the back of a young mother.

107

saves one from metaphysics, the Aztec, who were good herbalists, applied what they knew to ease the disease.

The cure doctor *(ticitl)* appeared in cases of serious illness; he brought with him all the appurtenances of the shaman (in the theatrical world "props")—shells, eagle wings, a hank of hair, tobacco to purify by smoke. He began as a masseuse by rubbing on the body to find and extract the "fairydart"—a stone, a rock, a small arrow—which had entered the body and "caused" the illness. One of the names of the cure doctor comes from this: *tetla-acuicili-que:* "he-who-recovers-the-stone." Illness was not natural; it had a mystical cause. It was carried down from the mountain on winds (we believed the tertiary fevers came from the bad air; hence: "mal-aria"); or *Tlaloc,* the rain-god, for a lack of proper obeisance, sent leprosy, ulcers, even foot trouble (a disaster to people who were their own dray animals); or if man and woman in love breached the tabu of incest, they could die of *tlazolmiquiztli,* "love death." The best cure for such cravings was to invoke the name of the genie of desire, one *Tlazol-teteo,* and take a hot steam bath (not much different from the method described in the limerick "by thinking of Jesus/and venereal diseases/ and the risk of begetting a child").

If the cause of the disease, after the magical object had been removed, was not easily diagnosed, the witch doctor gave the patient an infusion of the bark of *oloiuhqui.* Since this is of the *Datura* family and possesses narcotic properties, the patient dreamed and talked and supposedly revealed the cause of his illness. (The same principle underlies shock treatment in modern medicine.) Once the hocus-pocus was over, the cure doctor used remedies, some sensible, others ineffectual and still others (as in our own world) ridiculous and even harmful. Whatever it was, the Indian patient accepted it without protest, afraid to modify it by complaint and spoil its miraculous powers.

What were the diseases they had to cure? About the same as afflicted most of the indigenous "Americans" before white man's arrival: colds, grippe, and all the other respiratory diseases; malaria; swarms of intestinal infections and infestations; leprosy; skin diseases; and—most probably—syphilis.

The Aztec herbalists worked out a classification of plants, particularly of those having therapeutic value. Much of this information, fortunately, was gathered before time and the effect of conquest brought it to an end.

There are a few such herbals extant, for one the De la Cruz–Badiano *Aztec Herbal,* written in 1552 and edited by William Gates.[77]

The herbalist had a full command of curatives, as was known to José de Acosta, the learned Jesuit who traveled in Mexico in 1565: "I say onely that in the time of . . . the Mexican Kings, there were many great personages expert in curing of diseases with simples . . . having the knowledge of the many vertues and properties of hearbes, roots, woodes and plants. . . . There are a thousand of these simples fit to purge, as the rootes of *Guanucchoacan,* the *Pignons of Punua,* the conserve of *Guanucquo,* the oyle of Fig-trees . . ."

They were, like all such Homeric simples, formed of equal portions of cure, hope and magic. For boils take the leaves of the *tlatl-anquaye* root, apply morning and noon, wash after the application with urine. Loss of hair could be prevented by a lotion of dog's or deer's urine with the plant called *xiuh-amolli.* If the head was broken in battle "the break should be smeared with plants growing in summer dew, with green-stone pearls, crystal and the *tlaca-huatzin,* and with wormy earth, ground up in the blood from a bruised vein and the white of an egg; if blood cannot be had burned frogs will take the place." The cures suggest the disease that affected the Aztec: he ate overly of corn, too little meat, not enough green-stuffs; the tropics brought their toll of intestinal diseases; birth was not always as easy as it is made out to be.

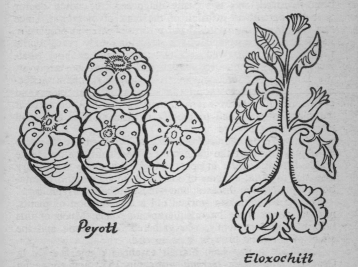

Peyotl

Eloxochitl

Fig. 37. Mexican medicinal plants. From an Aztec herbal.

Overheated eyes were cured by mixing the root of *matlal-xochitl* with mother's milk (note of warning: one suffering from this affection would abstain from sex and wear on his neck a red crystal and on his right arm the eye of a fox). Bloodshot eyes, cataract, tumors in the eyes, were all treated with plants that have been identified as having positive medicinal value. Colds, common or otherwise, catarrh, were helped by inhaling the odors of the plant *a-toch-ietl,* which is the "penny-royal" of commerce and is still used in some parts as a culicifuge.

Teeth, generally good, were ofttimes affected by swelling gums and toothache; the tooth was first punctured and a poultice made from the cactus *teonochtli* and farina then applied.

Tumors were cut out with obsidian knives and after surgery the crushed leaves of a plant were applied. "Lameness of the hands" was to be cured by steeping the hands in warm water where the leaves of a bitter astringent had been crushed, after which the patient was to put his hand on an ant nest and "let him patiently allow the lame hands to be bitten by the ants' pincers." Heart pains, burning of the heart, pains in the side, all of which came from overdrinking of the fermented *octli,* were treated with other herbs.

Stomach ailments were frequent among a people whose intestines swarmed with ankylostoma; medicines to kill stomach worms, tumors and cures for dysentery appear often in the herbal. The bladderwort, which the Aztec called *coa-nenepilli,* was used "when the flow of urine is shut off"; this was mixed with other bitter plants and "administered as an emetic." "If this medicine avails nothing," says the herbal, "it will be then necessary to take the pith of an extremely slender palm, covered with cotton, smeared with honey and crushed with the herb *huihuitz-mallotic* and this cautiously inserted into the virile member."

Gout, rectal infections, rheumatism ("pain in the knees"), were frequent. More so were "cracks in the soles of the feet" for those who walked and drayed all of their life. There were remedies for "black blood" fevers (of which there is a good diagnosis in the herbals: "spit blood, body jerks and turns hither and thither, he sees little"). Hemorrhoids were present, and not, as often supposed, the result of modern occupational stresses, but if one had to go through the Aztec cure, perhaps it would be best to be left with the hemorrhoids ("before the cure let him kill a weasel and eat it quite alone with dragon's blood"). Ringworm was endemic; the itch, dyspepsia and warts were all part of the trouble of living. For all, specific cures were offered. Those who were "fear-burdened" had only to take a drink of the potion made of the herb called *tonatiuh-yxiuh* mixed with other plants and make a poultice of it with the blood of a wolf, the blood and excrement of an *acuecue-yxoyalotl,* ground together with sea-foam.

Lice on the head, lousy distemper, and goatlike smell of the armpits could apparently be easily cured. There was much occupation with birth and many remedies were offered for recent parturition, to increase the flow of milk, and for breast tubercles. The herbalist relieved pain in childbirth but his methods would have appealed more to Jean Jacques Rousseau, who popularized the "noble savage," than to the gynecologist: "the womb of a woman entering childbirth is to be washed out with the juice of the plants. Into the womb you also inject the triturated herb *ayo nelhuatl* and eagle excrement. . . ."

There has been to date no comprehensive study of Aztec diseases. There is no evidence of surgery or of skull trephining, as in Peru. However, this negative evidence is not decisive since we have little skeletal remains of these peoples. There is little doubt, however, that Aztec herbal medicine was far advanced. Certainly a people who could offer a remedy to relieve "the fatigue of those administering government and discharging public offices" * must have had a vast pharmacopeia or else a good sense of humor.

Yet there came a time, as it does to all, when medicines were of no aid. From the time of a child's conception everyone in clan and tribe did his best to aid him through life; a mother was deflowered by others than the father so that evil, which was everywhere, would not harm him; at birth a priest had been called in to consult the auguries to be certain that

---

* The bark of the tree *quetzal-ylin,* the flowers of *elo-xochitl* and *izqui-xochitl,* the almond with its fruit, which is the *tlapal-cacahuatl,* the flowers *cacalo-xochitl, huacal-xochitl, meca-xochitl, huey nacaztli,* and all fine-smelling summer flowers, leaves of the trees *a-ylin, oyametl, ocotl, a-xocotl, eca-patli, tlaco-izqui-xochitl, quauh-yyauhtli, tomazquitl, ahuatl, tepe-ylin, ayauh-quahuitl,* and *te-papaquilti quahuitl,* flower-bearing plants with their shrubbery, which you gather before the wind rises; these are expressed one by one in clear spring water, into new vessels or vases. This then stays for a day and a night, when the *huitz-quahuitl* wood, with a red juice, is added as coloring.

Also the blood of wild animals, namely the red ocelot, *cuet-lachtli, miztli, ocotochtli,* white ocelot, *tlaco-ocelotl,* is sought for. With this and the above liquors the body is well anointed.

These medicaments healthily give gladiatorial strength to the body, drive fatigue far off and also cast out timidity and strengthen the human heart.

the child be named on a lucky day; from cradle to fatal illness the fear of the "things" that moved through the supersensuous world never left him. What one did or did not do was only an attempt to steer successfully between Scylla and Charybdis on this uncertain sea of life. When the end approached, the dying must have felt that not enough had been done to propitiate the unseen powers, perhaps somewhere along the way something had been forgotten, somewhere there had been a failure to conform.

Now that all had failed the dying knew that the understanding alone was not enough to comprehend the world; somewhere the arguments of the heart must stand. . . . The Aztec herbal gave final advice; the *ticitl,* "the cure-doctor—will draw his auguries as to whether the patient is to die or get well from the eyes and nose. . . . A mark of death is a sootiness found in the middle of the eyes . . . eyes growing dark and unseeing . . . nose getting thin. . . . Also ever grinding of the teeth . . . and finally the babbling of words without meaning . . . in the way of parrots. . . . You may anoint the chest with pine-wood crushed in water . . . or puncture the skin with a wolf's bone or that of an eagle or that of a puma . . . or you can hang close to the nostrils the heart of a kestrel wrapped in a deerskin. . . . If none of these avail, that fatal necessity is at hand . . . and death is complete."

José Limón

1. The Totonac, on the coast of Vera Cruz (where Cortés first landed), produced a wide and varied art: a clay Faustian bearded figure, with lined face, immense headgear.

Victor von Hagen

2. The celebrated laughing figures, molded, perhaps cast, from clay molds. These are typical of the Totonac area, but quite unique in all Mexico.

José Limón

3. Monte Albán: The pyramidal structure known as "M" which was begun in the first epoch of the temple-city (that is, 100 B.C.), and then reconstructed at various other periods, stands on the east side of the plaza, next to the Temple of the Dancers. It is surrounded by tall glyphed monoliths which, while not fully deciphered, suggest that they were set up during the occupation of the Mixtec, the traditional border enemies of the Zapotec, the first builders of the temple-city.

Victor von Hagen

4. Totonac: From the same hot tropic land that produced unusual stone sculptures and the temple-cities of Tajín, Papantla, Cempoala, comes this delicate clay figure. The rendering is as sensitive as anything out of Egypt.

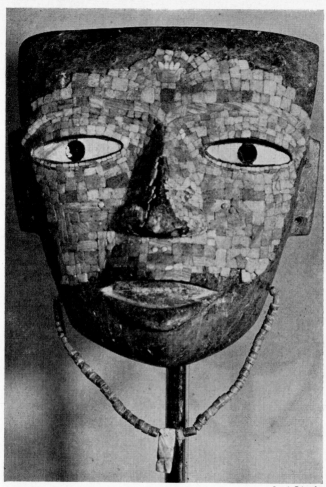

José Limón

5. A stone mask, covered with jade, from the tombs of Monte Albán, the sacred temple of the Mixtec. The eyes are of mother of pearl; the iris is a piece of volcanic obsidian-glass.

José Limón

6. The suspended movement of a clay Zapotec figurine. It is a dancing figure; bells hang about his calves, decorations such as the tongue speech-scrolls are about his neck.

7. Victor von Hagen at the ruins of Mitla (Zapotecan culture) in Oaxaca.

8. The geographical position of the Zapotec kingdom (midway between central Mexico and tropic hotlands of Chiapis) gave them
jade, of which this striking mask of the Bat-God is made.

9. Tula: A southern view of the enormous stone figures of Toltec warriors which formed part of the main temple of Tula. Note the face set within a rotary calendar which was tied about the waist of the warriors, and the details of the tied leg protection.

Victor von Hagen

10. Xochicalco: The façade of the Temple of Quetzalcoatl (north lateral) is completely covered with a frieze of open-fanged serpents, the tails of which are covered with plumes and are therefore the symbol of Quetzalcoatl, the Plumed Serpent. As there are many Toltec elements in the decoration, and as Xochicalco lies only 100 miles south of Teotihuacán, it is at present believed to have been related to the Central American cultures.

Victor von Hagen

11. Xochicalco: Detail of the plumed serpent motif of the façade of the Temple of Quetzalcoatl.

Victor von Hagen

12. The ascending steps of the Temple of the Sun at Teotihuacán. Artificially raised, this pyramid became the standard method of displaying the dignity of the gods.

Silvia von Hagen

13. Another view of the Temple of the Sun at Teotihuacán.

José Limón

14. An example of the curious original motifs in low-relief on jade, from the Olmec of Tabasco. The Olmec are presumed to have been the cultural intermediary between the Maya and Central Mexico.

José Limón

15. The humorous art forms of the Tarascans: An old traveler with stick and fish-feet. The Tarascans were contemporaneous with the Aztec. Their area—the modern states of Jalisco and Colima—was adjacent to that of the Aztec.

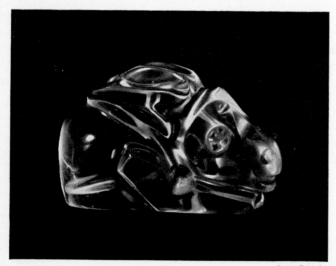

José Limón

16. Aztec: A rabbit, carved from a piece of translucent quartz.

José Limón

17. Aztec: A vase with a crouching figure, fashioned from the hard, brittle, volcanic obsidian.

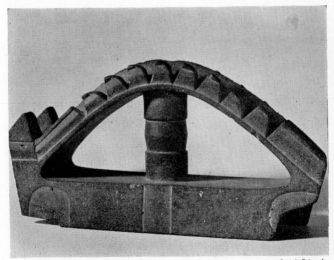

José Limón

18. A piece of superbly polished stone, perhaps representing a bridge under which boats (the main Aztec transport) passed in Tenochtitlán.

José Limón

19. Aztec: Xipe, the flayed goddess, accoutered in the skin of a freshly killed sacrificial victim. The priests danced in such skin-costumes. Here the artist has immortalized it.

José Limón

20. The flayed goddess, Xipe, from the back. A graphic picture of how the skin was tied in knots to the body of another.

José Limón

21. Aztec drums: two-tongued and noted drums used in dances, religious and ceremonial processions. A figure on the wall suggests the technique of playing. Left, a wooden drum from Tlaxcala, and lower right, two drums in pottery form.

Printed in U.S.A.

22. The Undead

"It is a fact," someone says in *The Magic Mountain*, "that a man's dying is more the survivors' affair than his own"; it certainly was a fact to the Aztec. Death complicated everything. The survivors had to do penance in many ways for the unsocial act of their kinsman's dying. Does death put an end to us utterly and entirely? The Aztec did not know how to answer this. They had not the subtlety of the French poet who answered the question by saying: *"Je suis, elle n'est pas; elle est, je ne suis plus."* "To the Aztec," writes Jacques Soustelle, "death and life were but aspects of the same reality." [78] He could not (any more than you and I) imagine himself as "not being."

Then came the "confession"; it is as ancient as man's society. The dying had to confess; it is a very important part of Christian religious and communistic political behavior patterns; it goes back to a far-reaching primitivity. Confessions had a virtue of their own; they were essential to neutralize the evil influences brought on by dying. For example, the Aztec believed that the act of dying caused uncleanliness (for dying is a form of social defilement). There actually existed a mystic bond, some sort of participation like that which unites a living man and his belongings. Man is responsible, he is the silent accomplice of the evil which is being propagated. He must confess; the sorcerer was called in to attend to it.

He arrived, consulted the sacred roll, and tobacco smoke was blown across the dying man; invocations were made to the gods so that he would die like an Aztec of good sense; then they prepared the body for burial. First in his mouth a green stone to take the place of his heart. It was not as the obolus which the Greeks put into the mouth of the dead to pay the passage across the river Styx; rather it was a heart-symbol—the "Heart of Jade"—for his journey to the unworld. Food was prepared, drink put in bowls, and the mummy bundle made complete. The next step was inhumation. Two courses were open to the Aztec for the disposal of the dead, but the choice really depended on social position. If he was a common Indian the body was swathed in cloth, tied with a cord, and festooned with paper flags; funeral chants *(micca-cuicatl)* were put into the mouths of the dead by the living:

> Where shall I go?
> Where shall I go?
> The road of the god of duality.
> Is your house perchance in the place of the fleshless?
> Perchance inside heaven?
> or here on earth only
> is the place of the fleshless?

Death stirs most, primitive or civilized, for to die (at least to the Aztec) was to accomplish an act of incalculably far-reaching potentialities. The dead were in reality living, they had merely passed from one phase to another, they were invisible, impalpable, invulnerable. The dead, or, better, in their feeling, the *undead,* had become the unseen members of the clan. The body of the common man, swathed in cloth, tied into a death-bundle, had things of his life and other things for his death-life journey. He was then cremated and the ashes were put into a pot on which the piece of jade was placed; the pot was kept in the house.

Cremation was general except where those of elevated rank were concerned; the leaders were entombed. The "Anonymous Conquistador" [79] found one of them after the rape of Mexico-Tenochtitlán. He found a mummy sitting with his personal device, sword and jewels amounting to "3,000 castellanos."

The departed went to those tutelary genii who had protected them in life; the knights of the eagles, warriors and valiant women (considered the same as warriors) went to the land of Tlaloc, the rain-god; he also cordially received those souls who died by drowning, since he was the god of water. How one acted or did not act in life had no relation to one's degree of immortality; conduct in life did not determine the soul's place in the shades. "The vertical world," says Dr. Vaillant, "was divided into heavens and hells [there were 13 heavens and 9 hells] which had no moral significance." It was one's occupation in life and manner of dying that determined it: warriors went to the eastern paradise, flower-filled; women who died in childbirth went into a western paradise and came to earth to haunt children and women in unspent spleen. Those of the undead who were unclassified made the passage to Mictlan; this was a veritable *via dolorosa;* rivers to cross, mountains to climb, deserts to cross, enduring of freezing winds and rain; the dead needed all the charms that the survivors put among the funeral pyre to provide talismans for the journey. When the soul arrived at the realm of the Lord of the Dead he was assigned to one of the nine hells; the piece of green stone tied to the mouth when the cadaver was swathed was left as a pledge in the seventh hell. Poor human beings, we must needs furnish ourselves with illusions even in death. Since man, primitive or civilized, cannot endure the idea of a mechanistic interpretation of the universe, no more can he grasp the fact that when one is not, one ceases to be. Ignorance is not alone a necessary condition of happiness, it is a condition of life itself; the sentiments that make life bearable to all spring out of falsehood and are fed on illusions. "We do not believe," said the Aztec, "we fear."

Meanwhile, the living must go into mourning for eighty days. There were a variety of impositions and tabus on food, dress and indulgence in sex; sustenance had to be regularly placed at the death urn, prayers given, blood offered from cuts made in the ears and tongue. All must be done to obtain the goodwill of the recent dead; their displeasure could have dire consequences and could expose the living to twofold retribution: from the justly-offended recently dead and from fellow clan-members, who collectively would have to suffer the consequences of the dead's anger. After eighty days the tabu was lifted. It was repeated on and off for four years; ". . . it is a fact that a man's dying is more the survivors' affair than his own. . . ."

Such, from womb to tomb, was the daily life of the Aztec common man; he was the base of the pyramid of Aztec society. Higher up in rank by election there were the clan heads; these in turn had representation on the tribal council (*tecuhtli*), and at the top of this curious melange of elected officials were the "council of four" (*tlatoani*). Finally at the apex was the semidivine chief speaker, the *Uei Tlatoani* (also elected), head of the army, high priest, the court of last appeal in the city-state of Tenochtitlán.

The well-remembered "king" Moctezuma was the Uei Tlatoani in that fateful year of 1519.

III

THE AZTEC "KINGS"
AND THE DIRECTING CLASSES

23. Moctezuma

The ruler of the Aztec had as title "One Who Speaks" (derived from the verb *tlatoa,* to speak); he was elected. So William Prescott was not entirely incorrect in calling their form of government an "elective monarchy." He was not absolute, as in the Peruvian theocracy; he did not claim ownership of the land, the earth, the people, as did the Inca; the Aztec were in theory democratic.[80] Each family was a member of a soil community; a cluster of these families formed a clan, of which twenty made up the tribe of the Tenochas. Each clan had its own council and an elected leader; of these the oldest or wisest or more experienced were selected to make up a council, and these were the link between the clans and the tribe's governing body. This council was narrowed down to four principals, who were advisers to the leader of state and, as well, electors of the "king" (functioning, to pursue a convenient analogy, as did the electors of the Holy Roman Empire), since "kings" were not such by primogeniture and were selected from the brothers of the previous ruler, or, if he had none, from his nephews, by the "four." These *tlatoani* were the key figures in Aztec government; they chose that "noble" descendant who in their mind was most distinguished in valor, war, knowledge. Such a one was Moctezuma, who was "crowned" in 1503. There is a description of him which is the most penetrating we have of any such ruler of any of the Sun Kingdoms of ancient America.

It was November 18, 1519, when Hernán Cortés arrived with his small army at Tenochtitlán, where two causeways coalesced. "Here nearly 1,000 of the chief citizens came out to greet me, all dressed alike and richly; on coming to speak

116

Fig. 38. Moctezuma Xocoyotzin—Moctezuma II, the younger (reigned 1503–20). As "First Speaker" he ruled Mexico when it reached its apogee. Although the materials of his clothes were finer, basically they were the same style as his subjects: cloak, breechclout and sandals. The headgear is his "crown."

with me each performed a ceremony very common to them, to wit, placing his hand on the ground and then kissing it, so that for nearly an hour I stood while they performed this ceremony.

"Moctezuma himself came out to meet us with some two hundred nobles. . . . They came forward in two long lines keeping close to the walls of the street. . . . Moctezuma was borne along in the middle of the street with two lords, one on his right and left. . . . Moctezuma wore sandals, whereas the others were barefoot."

Bernal Díaz, who had not to content himself with lofty political remarks, kept to description where Cortés left off. "The Great Moctezuma was about forty years old, of good height and well proportioned, slender and spare of flesh, not very swarthy but of the natural colour and shade of an Indian. He did not wear his hair long . . . his scanty beard was well-shaped and thin. His face was somewhat long but cheerful. . . . He was very neat and clean and bathed once every afternoon. He had many women as mistresses, daughters of Chieftains, and he had two great Cacicas as his legitimate wives. He was free from unnatural offences [that is, sodomy]. The clothes that he wore one day, he did not put on again until four days later [the Lord-Inca never wore the same garment twice]; he had 200 Chieftains in his guard . . . and when they went to speak to him they were obliged to take off their rich mantles and put on others of little worth . . . to enter barefoot with eyes lowered to the ground and not to look at his face . . . and they made him three obeisances." (The Lord-Inca imposed a similar ritual.)

Moctezuma ate like a grand vizier. "For each meal over thirty different dishes were prepared . . . and they placed small pottery braziers beneath the dishes so that they should not get cold. He had such a variety of dishes . . . turkeys, pheasants, partridges, quail, ducks, venison, wild boar, pigeons, hares . . . so numerous that I cannot finish naming them." Moctezuma sat "on a low stool soft and richly worked. . . . Four very beautiful cleanly women brought water for his hands . . . in a *xical*-gourd . . . and two women brought him tortilla-bread and as soon as he began to eat they placed before him a sort of wooden screen painted over with gold so that no one could watch him eating. . . . Four great chieftains [these were the *tlatoani*] who were old men came and stood beside him and conversed. . . . They say that these elders were his near relations and were his counsellors . . . They brought him fruit of all different kinds . . . and from time to time in cup-shaped vessels of the purest gold, a certain drink made from cacao. . . . Sometimes at meal-times there were present some very ugly humpbacks . . . who are their jesters and other Indians, who must have been buffoons.

"There were also placed on the table three tubes, painted and gilded, which held liquid amber mixed with certain herbs which they called tobacco and when he had finished eating . . . he inhaled the smoke from one of these tubes . . . with that he fell asleep."

Moctezuma became a demigod. Although elected, with leadership he took on semidivinity. He was high priest, supreme commander of the army, and head of state, a plenary ruler, advised by council, with his power only held in check by ancient mores. Moctezuma was the ninth in succession, the nephew of the last ruler, Ahuitzotl, and grandson of Moctezuma I (surnamed "The Wrathy"). As an Aztec ruler-aspirant he was trained like all such in the "religious" schools, the *calmecac* ("house of the large corridors"). There, with the image of Quetzalcoatl painted on the wall, he learned by means of glyphic charts the history of the Tenochas. He was taught to read glyph writing, remember the list of dates of rulers and history, which succinctly was:

Aztec history begins	A.D. 1168
Tenochtitlán settled	A.D. 1325

List of Aztec realm leaders after A.D. 1375:

Acampichtli	ruled	1375–1395
Huitzilhuitl	„	1395–1414
Chimalpopoca	„	1414–1428
Itzcoatl	„	1428–1440
Moctezuma I	„	1440–1469
Axayacatl	„	1469–1481
Tizoc	„	1481–1486
Ahuitzotl	„	1486–1503
Moctezuma II	„	1503–1520

He studied the use of Aztec arms, swords, slings and arrows, for it was expected he would be a military leader; once he knew and understood ideographic writing he learned about the stars, astrology, calendar, and through constant reading of the *tonalamatl* (used as an aid in memory) he learned the rituals and interpretation of phenomena. As a youth Moctezuma had taken a very active part in the wars; later he devoted much attention to religion, "scrupulous in his attentions to all the burdensome ceremonial of the Aztec worship." José de Acosta said that he was "grave and staid and spake little, so when hee gave his opinion . . . then he was feared and respected. . . . Hee marched with such gravitie . . . they all sayd the name of Moctezuma ['Courageous Lord'] agreed very well with his nature."

When elected Moctezuma was found sweeping down the 133 steps of the great temple of Huitzilopochtli ("to show that he desired not the Emprey," adds Acosta in an aside). "The electors . . . giving him notice that hee was chosen king . . . he was ledde before the harth of their gods . . . where he offered sacrifice in drawing blood from his eares & the calves of his legges."

First, war, where he went in person to an enterprise "necessary for his coronation," i.e., prisoners for sacrifice. He moved down to the Gulf, extended Aztec domination in both directions, and returned in triumph to Mexico and had his nose septum pierced for insertion of the royal emerald for his coronation. The number of sacrificial victims did not quite reach that of his uncle's piety; Ahuitzotl had immolated twelve thousand.

Moctezuma was "crowned" with a sort of miter; the color symbol of his power was blue-green. Immediately after coming to power he turned out the rankless people about him, commanding that "only the most noble and most famous men of his realme shoulde live within his pallace," thus severing the democratic base of "first speaker"; it had been "custome" to have people of all shades and hues about the royal rooms ever since the time of "king" Itzcoatl, who had been born of a slave-concubine in his father's house. Moctezuma seems to have taken on some of the prerogatives of a god; whether this was done before him by other "chief speakers" is not made clear.

Dress for Moctezuma was like the lower man's except that it was more elaborate. He wore the breechclout, elaborate sandals, the manta (*tilmantli*), and all the other accouterments so highly praised by the conquerors. These descriptions by the Spaniards, which were later dismissed by eighteenth-century historians as inspired by the heady fumes of war, have been confirmed by archaeology. Few—outside of the Maya kingdom—lived as sumptuously; the apparent overdrawing is no exaggeration of the real splendor of it all.

Marriage for the "first gentleman of the realm" was basically no different from the "tying of the *tilmantli*" among the lower orders, but, like royal marriages everywhere, it was often an alliance. There was one legitimate wife (although Bernal Díaz says two); the Spanish historian Oviedo elicited from

Doña Isabel, one of the legitimate daughters of Moctezuma, that he had 150 children by his various concubines, but confirmed that he had only one legitimate wife. She was the executive; all others took orders from her; indeed, our terms "legitimate" and "illegitimate" had no meaning. The numerous progeny were trained for office. This is true of all polygamous marriages; the Inca used his enormous offspring as sources for leadership in the realm and the Aztec practiced a similar nepotism. Nezahualpilli, "king" of Texcoco, allied to Mexico, "had more than 2,000 concubines"; [81] in a society where war took men's lives faster than they could be created by simple monogamous birth, polygyny seemed most functional; besides nothing so favors a marriage and consequently social stability as the indulgence of temporary polygamy.

Moctezuma ruled well; he spread the realm farther than all others before him, tribute was collected from 371 towns, justice in particular was well organized by him. "If there were any excesse of defect he did then punish it rigorously. . . . And also to discern how his ministers did execute their officers he often disguised himselfe . . . if they offended, they were punished. Besides that he was a great justicier and very noble, he was very valiant and happy . . . and he obtained great victories and came to his greatness." But the times were out of joint: the heavens and the hells rose to plague him. What we would call natural phenomena, to them was evil omen: it snowed in Mexico; the volcano Popocatepetl, which had lain quiescent for time's age, became active; a child was born with two heads; the king of Texcoco (he of the 2,000 women), who was a "greate Magitian," came over one day "at an extraordinary hour" to tell him that the gods had revealed he would lose his whole realm. To give it all a sense of history, Quetzalcoatl, who had declared against human sacrifice and was the cultural hero of these lands, had sailed away in exile into the Atlantic saying that he would again return in the same year of his birth to "reestablish my rule." His birth had been in the Aztec year 1-Reed (*ce-acatl*); in the Aztec calendar this could only fall in the years 1363, 1467—and 1519. For years Moctezuma had all but given up the military direction of his government and was surrounded by a corps of astrologers, augurs, necromancers, and mediums from whom he sought by the interpretation of signs, symbols and observation of the portents to learn what to do to win back the favor of the gods.

What had happened was simple enough: white men had reached America's shores. In 1502, one year before Moctezuma's coronation, Cristóbal Colón, on his fourth and last voyage, had made contact with the Maya; it did not take long for this event to boil over from the Maya councils and be carried over the trails from people to market and from tribe to tribe. Later, Yañez Pinzón and Juan Díaz de Solís skirted the shores of Yucatan, and once again rumor as it were sniffed the breeze, traveled over the jungles, and somewhere was set down by a glyph-writer to be sent to Moctezuma: "strange bearded men in large boats came from out of the ocean-sea."

No "king" in Aztec history had so terrible a problem to cope with as Moctezuma.

24. Rule and Organization

The rule and organization of Tenochtitlán were through the system already adumbrated: the "king," Uei Tlatoani, gave his desires to the "council of four"; they in turn conveyed it to the larger body of clan heads (*teuchtli*), then down to the clan body, where another official, who enforced peace and was the clan leader during a war, gave to members of the clan the programs promulgated from the higher reaches.

This clan, the basic unit, as aforesaid, of the system, enforced clan peace, organized for war, rounded out clan taxation; orders through these methods reached down to the very last rung of the social ladder. It seems that the Aztec did not administer the affairs of conquered peoples. Perhaps they were not interested in doing so. The Inca in Peru had a system of sending *mitimaes,* a "safe" population of Quechua-speaking peoples, into newly conquered lands and removing the unsafe newly conquered. By this system the Inca conquered and amalgamated that which they conquered. The Aztec had no such system. They imposed a tribute, not excessive, except for sacrificial victims, a contribution which fitted into the conquerors' economy. This was brought every six months to Tenochtitlán. Still the Aztec won no friends and forged no empire. They went through all the social evolution of Neolithic states everywhere: passed from land where first all worked at agriculture, to city which became temple-city, where a social surplus produced non-farmers, specialists in architecture, sculpture, lapidaries and priest-craft, people who themselves no longer grew food. Then their society passed into the city-state with satellite towns, and Tenochtitlán developed an extended priestly class who exacted "first fruits" for the temples. Then lastly it became the conquering and finally the tribute-city.

There were enough reasons for this. The Aztec were fighting people. They had no luxuries on their land: cotton, brilliant bird feathers, chocolate, gold, rubber, were not of their earth's bounty. If they wanted these things, they got them by conquest. Moreover, as they became specialized they manufactured and traded. It was difficult enough: each region was hostile to every other; there were few natural avenues; imbroglios had to be called off so trading could be carried on. There was a great lack of unity even among towns nominally Aztec. As Tenochtitlán, the conquering city, widened its horizons, new products, new ideas, came into it and gradually luxuries were converted into necessities.

Trade became vital to Mexico and war was continuous; tribute, the result of conquest, poured in from all over many far-flung places and was distributed among the clans. As this gave people more leisure from the fields, leisure was devoted to manufacture, which in turn produced articles they traded for luxuries at the market. A new class of merchant (*pochteca*) came into being—a phenomenon in ancient America: traders who had their own guilds, their own gods, and were above the laws that applied to most. They set out from Mexico periodically with long trains of human carriers (*tamenes*), 60 pounds on their backs, preceded by the lordly *pochteca*. Protected in disputed terrain by soldiers, the human caravans penetrated into southern Mexico, into and beyond Guatemala, down as far as Nicaragua. They traded Aztec manufactures for the raw products of the hotlands: emeralds, which slowly found their way from Muzo in Colombia (the only place they were found in pre-Hispanic America), gold from Panama, feathers from Guatemala, jaguar skins, eagle feathers, cotton, chocolate, chicle, rubber, live birds for the royal aviary in Mexico (the source of plumage for the feather weavers). Roads of a sort were opened, Aztec garrisons were placed at strategic places or among the newly conquered; the *pochteca* moved freely.

There is a natural limit to conquest. The Aztec had no definite plan of assimilation. Conquest often followed trade as the Aztec got information on riches and defenses brought back by the merchants; sometimes the process went the other way: villages city-states, subjected to sharp wars of conquest were made to yield tribute. This expanded until at the time of Moctezuma there were 371 such.

So during the growth of Aztec power all the riches of all these cultures were pouring into their capital.

Mexico-Tenochtitlán was an island and a watery city.

It was something like Venice. There was the same type of *calli* and *campis*, with hundreds of meandering streets, filled with canals, bridges and dikes. This Tenochtitlán began as

Fig. 39. Mexico-Tenochtitlán as it would have appeared to an Aztec artist. The plan is schematic, but seen in the center is the great temple, the *teocalli;* about it was the main plaza. To the north was Tlatelolco, a rival city, until it was subjugated by swift conquest and made a part of greater Mexico.

Venice, not out of "feelings of men" who founded cities, but out of safety. Just as the primitive Venetians took possession of the tide-washed sandbanks in the Adriatic, and turned this undefined swampy tract into a city with its canals and waterways, so did the Aztec, fleeing the mainland, seek safety on the two marsh-bound islets three miles from shore on Lake Texcoco.

Tenochtitlán was named after a cactus, *tenochtli,* which grew on the islet; the people became the Tenocha, the city Tenochtitlán. The name broken into radicals shows its origin: *tetl,* "rock," *nochtli,* "cactus," *tlan,* "place of." An eagle is supposed to have perched on the cactus during the founding; however, one of the Ten who, according to legend, founded the city was called "Tenoch"; it could be that this gave the city its name.

The oval-shaped valley of Anáhuac at 7,244 feet altitude held the waters of the lakes, 30 by 50 miles, and was identified by five separate names; a contiguous body of water, varying from fresh to saline, the largest was Texcoco. Directly out from Chapultepec forest, three miles more or less ("seven leagues" said Hernán Cortés), there were two islets, rock outcrops surrounded by mudbanks and reed-fringed. This was the base of Tenochtitlán.

The first buildings were structures of wattle and daub, the "immortal" house even today of the upland peasant. Then followed the temple, which, rebuilt from century to century, grew into the awesome Temple of Huitzilopochtli (the present site of Mexico's Cathedral). While developing the two islets * the Aztec apparently by treaty maintained some foothold for cultivation on the mainland, augmenting this by the ingenious *chinampa,* the "floating garden," and the space between these formed the canals. Centuries of these operations enlarged the original mud flats until "Greater Mexico-Tenochtitlán," that is, Tenochtitlán and Tlatelolco, formed a city 1¾ miles square and containing upwards of 2,500 acres. This was a sizable area: Rome's walls at the time of Marcus Aurelius enclosed a city of only 3,500 acres; London town in the time of Samuel Pepys was scarcely any larger.

Mexico-Tenochtitlán as a city grew as Venice grew: the Aztec raided the land about the lakes—a conquest here, a land treaty there—until by A.D. 1400 most of the city-states and their lands were under Aztec domination. Their safety

* There were two islets; one, Tlatelolco, had been occupied by Aztec warriors coming over from adjacent Atzacoalco on the mainland; Tenochtitlán was settled by those coming from Chapultepec. The two grew up rivals as Buda and Pest or Minneapolis and St. Paul. A bridge connected them. Rivalry led to war in 1473; Tlatelolco was conquered and incorporated into Greater Mexico.

assured, they began to build the great causeways that connected the island-kingdom to the mainland. There were four; the best and most authentic description of them is by Hernán Cortés, the man who destroyed the city.

"The great city of Tenochtitlán . . . is 2 leagues [5 miles] . . . to any point on the mainland. Four causeways lead to it . . . some 12 feet wide." The one which he took to enter the city in 1519 began at Iztalalapa ("where we saw so many cities and villages built in the water and other great towns on dry land and that straight and level Causeway," says Bernal Díaz going towards Mexico). This causeway ("as broad as two lances and broad enough for eight horsemen to ride abreast") went for about a mile and there made junction with another causeway coming from the city of Coyoacan. Here there was a fort with battlements and a drawbridge, then the causeway went on some two miles directly north to the city. It was much used, "as broad, yet so crowded with people that there was hardly room for them all." The second was an auxiliary causeway with aqueduct, which arched in a curve connected with some part of the mainland and entered this main causeway close to the entrance of the city. The third went westward toward Chapultepec (branching off to Tlacopan), i.e., Tacuba. This carried the aqueduct to the heart of the city. "Along . . . [this] causeway 2 pipes are constructed of masonry, each 2 paces broad [6 feet] and about as high as a man; one of which conveys a stream of water very clear and fresh." The other one lay empty to be used when the first was being cleaned. As the causeway had at intervals removable bridges in case of attack, the fresh water conduit, as explained by Hernán Cortés, "flows into a kind of [ceramic] trough as thick as an ox [25-inch conduit], which occupies the whole of the bridge." * The fourth and last causeway, the shortest, not much over a half mile in length, connected the city with the mainland at Tepeyacac.

This system of causeways, the greatest engineering feat of the Aztec, had a twofold purpose: communications and dike-levy. The lakes were subject to rise and fall; rain could raise the level rapidly (there was no outlet); wind could raise huge waves which lapped up to and over the city; it was subject to frequent inundations (as it is still today). As Tenochtitlán had almost been destroyed by flood in 1440, the then reigning Moctezuma I applied to his friend and ally, the ruler of the advanced city-state of Texcoco. The system of causeway-dikes was constructed in such a fashion as to contain the

* There were 2 aqueducts: one built by Ahuitzol (reigned 1486–1503), which went from Coyoacan over the arched causeway; it also emptied into a fountain in the main square.

waters of Lake Xochimilco; moreover, by breaking up the lakes with other causeway dikes, the freshness of Xochimilco's water was preserved and Mexico-Tenochtitlán was protected from the rise of the water level. As much of the lake was shallow (6 feet), the causeways were doubtless first pontooned and later replaced with *chinampas* firmly anchored to the shallows. With all their records the Aztec left us nothing illustrating their one great engineering feat.

The city, like Cuzco, capital of the Inca in Peru, was divided into four sections, corresponding to the causeways, which entered the city from three of the four cardinal directions. Each formal entrance to the city proper had a road block, where taxes were collected.

The view along the street, after it ceased to be a causeway, was clear and unobstructed ("one can see from one end to the other, though it is some 2 miles in length"), and both sides of the streets were lined with houses ("very beautiful, very large, both private dwellings and temples"). House styles varied with the rank of the owner. Those of lower position were constructed with walls of wattle and smeared with mud, grass thatched; those of rank were raised on a stone platform (in case of flood) made of sun-dried brick, plastered over and brilliantly colored.

The ordinary house, invariably one-storied and with pitched straw roof, had its postern to the street, a patio garden within, and by its narrow canal, the entrance; also a jetty for the

Fig. 40. The maguey plant (Aztec *metl*), and the method of gathering the sweet sap of the plant and storing it until it becomes fermented *octli*. This was one of the Aztec beverages.

dugout canoe. The principal houses were two-storied, made of *tezontli*-stone, with flat roofs. The city "had many wide and handsome streets," said the "Anonymous Conqueror"; they were in all probability of adobe, since to him they were "formed half of hard earth like a brick pavement." Many if not most of these "streets" were waterways, canals such as in Venice; "there are principal streets, entirely of water which can only be traversed by canoes." Each dwelling had a small plot of earth, a garden; this is evident in the fragment of an Aztec map (made circa 1480) drawn on *amatl*-paper and showing very clearly the individual houses, ground plots, streets and the great waterways.

Tenochtitlán was divided into twenty sections (*calpulli*); these the Spaniards called *barrios* (wards); we refer to them as clans. Each clan had its own *teocalli* (temple), and its school; each *calpulli* its name and emblem (coat of arms). In the largest of the squares was the great pyramid to Huitzilopochtli and Tlaloc. The 200-foot-high structure was double-stepped and double-templed; that on the left, painted white and blue, was to the national god, the Hummingbird Wizard; the other, white with blood-red background, was that of the rain-god and it very much impressed the Spanish. "It is one," wrote Hernán Cortés, "whose size and magnitude no human tongue can describe" although Padre Acosta tried to do so). "Upon the toppe of the Temple were two . . . Chappells and in them were two Idolls." The structures rested on a 40-foot square, for the pyramids, like all in Mexico, were truncated. Bernal Díaz ascended the great pyramid and counted the steps—114 within the temples, where Cortés and Moctezuma had their famous discourse on the value of gods; the roof beams and the stone were beautifully worked; it was so sacrosanct that few could enter and when Cortés wanted to dislodge them and plant a cross in their stead Moctezuma cut short the visit, saying "he had to pray and offer certain sacrifices on account of the grave *tatacul,* that is to say, sin, which he had committed for allowing us to see his great Cue." Near to the steps was the large sacrificial stone; Bernal Díaz shuddered to think of it: "They put the poor Indians for sacrifice, and there was an image like a Dragon . . . and much blood." *

* Bernal Díaz described the view from the top of that "huge and cursed temple." "We saw three causeways . . . that of Tzapalapa by which we entered Mexico . . . Tacuba and that of Tepeaquilla; we saw the fresh water that comes from Chapultepec [over the Tlacopan-Tacuba] causeway . . . we saw the bridges . . . we saw the temples and oratories like towers and fortresses all gleaming white, it was a wonderful thing to behold . . . the houses with flat roofs."

The stone-paved great plaza measured, as do the boundaries of the *zócalo* of present-day Mexico, 520 by 600 feet, and within that square there was the Great *Teocalli,* with four lesser pyramids on its several sides; the Temple of Quetzalcoatl, a rounded structure entwined with green open-fanged serpents; a raised dais on which gladiators fought; the sacred ball court, with, on one side, the residence of the officiating priests and, on the other, the house of the military order of the Eagles, an elite warrior class. The *tzompantli,* or skull rack, on which hung the craniums of the sacrificial victims, was close to the ball court. Three causeways terminated in the main square (just as in Cuzco, the capital of the Inca, the roads of "four quarters" that ran the length and breadth of their land terminated or began in the main plaza); of these, Ixtapalapa was the southern road and causeway, by which the Spanish also made their entry. The water entered the city at the great square and was from there either piped off to other sections or was gathered, as one still sees women today gather it, in water jugs. The city, gleaming white in the sun, with barbarically colored houses and temples, surrounded by the blue lake, must have appeared to be a floating city, something out of the *Thousand and One Nights,* with its gardens and aviaries and multitudes of people, giving it a life as orderly as a termitary; and so it seemed to Bernal Díaz: "We were amazed and said it was like the enchantments they tell of in the legend of Amadis." The impression that the city made was so lasting that even when this same Bernal Díaz was eighty-four years old, half blind, half deaf, aching from the old wounds and having nothing for all his time and effort, he could still write: "It was indeed wonderful and now that I am writing about it, it all comes before my eyes as if it had happened only yesterday."

The other half of the great square, empty of buildings, was the market, *tiaquiz.* Here the people were addressed by the "directing classes"; at one end was the sacred stone of war where the captains met before going off to do battle; at the other end was the calendar stone; in front of this was the new palace of Moctezuma. It was an immense structure, as large in area as the plaza, a virtual city in itself (the nineteenth-century modern Ayuntamiento occupies the same area today); it repeated the features of the great square in miniature. Two stories in height, Moctezuma's living quarters were on the second floor. The rest of the magnificent structure was honeycombed with rooms. There were sumptuous quarters for the "kings" of the city-state of Texcoco and Tlacopan to which the Aztec were allied; there were other rooms for at least three hundred accompanying guests, always coming and going. Below there were the tribunals, especially for those held until given trial, rooms for the "judges" *(achcauhcalli),* the public repository *(petalcalco)* where all the tribute from the 371 tribute towns was delivered and stored for distribution. It is to one of these rooms that Bernal Díaz was conducted to see the tribute. "There was a great Cacique . . . and he kept the accounts of all the revenue that was brought to Moctezuma and he kept it in his account books . . . and he had a great house full of every sort of arms . . . and in other quarters, cotton, foodstuffs, chocolate, feathers, gold, jewels, all that was part of the tribute-economy." In other sections were the rooms of the administrators who kept record of the economy of the theo-democracy.

On the second floor were the rooms of Moctezuma's wife, his 150 concubines and their offspring, his hundreds of guards and attendants. "Every morning at dawn," said Cortés, "there were over 600 nobles and chief men present in his palace, some of whom were seated, others walking around the rooms. . . . The servants of these nobles filled two or three courtyards and overflowed into the street."

The rooms were decorated amazingly with carved cedar beams which "could not be bettered anywhere," said stout Cortés, "for they were cut with ornamental borders of flowers, birds and fish." The walls were presumably adorned with hangings. Bernal Díaz and his "merrie boyes" were lodged in the Palace of Ayayactl, near to Moctezuma's palace on the square, and the "great halls and chambers were canopied with the cloth of the country . . . [the walls] coated with shining cement and swept and garlanded." Moctezuma's was decorated with murals and bas-reliefs, with door hangings and so many rooms and doors that the "Halls of Moctezuma" seemed like a labyrinth, at least to one Spaniard, who confessed: "I entered it more than four times, and there was always more and more to see and always I grew weary from walking and for this I was never able to see everything."

Attached to the palace, or within it (for it was full of patios), was the royal aviary. This astounded the conquistadors, for there was no zoo in Europe—they were unheard of. "There were ten pools of water in which they kept every kind of waterfowl known in these parts . . . and I can vouch for it to Your Majesty," wrote Cortés to Carlos V, fearful that if he described such a thing as an aviary the king would think him mad, "I can vouch that these birds, who only eat fish, receive some 250 pounds daily."

How large was the city, how large the fief of the city-state of Tenochtitlán? No one knew. Cortés admitted that he was "unable to find out the exact extent of . . . the kingdom." He thought it "as large as Spain." Certainly, even taking natural exaggeration into account, it was one of the world's largest cities; few of the temple-cities in the Old World seem to have been as large.

Of course it was not unique; ". . . a very unusual conjunction of circumstances," said V. Gordon Childe,[82] "which occurred at most five times—in the Tigris-Euphrates delta, in the Nile Valley, in the Indus Basin, in Mexico, Central America, and . . . Peru." Neolithic peoples depended wholly on agriculture, went through what he has called "The Urban Revolution," changed their social structure radically, both psychologically and economically, by intensifying the exploitation of the land, creating social surplus, freeing many from agricultural work and creating the full-time specialist; the city with all its complexities was the result. People crowding into cities was a radical departure from the "American pattern," where, either because of a basically unsocial nature or because of the extravagant methods of Neolithic cultivation—vast tracts of land were needed—clans or families were separated by considerable distances and only came together when the need was general.

How populous was ancient Tenochtitlán? The conquistadors said there were between 70,000 and 100,000 inhabited houses on the island-kingdom; if each house had between four and ten inhabitants, averaging 6 to the house, the population would have been about one-half million. Cortés's small army of 1,000 men, even with his Indian auxiliaries, could not have beaten down *that* number. "Read 8,000 instead of 80,000 houses," said Juan de Rivera, who, though he cheated at cards, tried to rob Cortés, and, to top it all, was cross-eyed; so was nevertheless a keen observer and doubted the figures; so did Bernal Díaz. One historian gives 30,000 for Mexico-Tenochtitlán,[83] but a modern French authority often quoted in this book falls back on the old figures; he says that the city had "a population certainly more than 500,000 and probably inferior to 1,000,000." [84]

The population of a historyless people is like the metaphysics of finance: it depends on how one reads the statistics.

Hernán Cortés should have known; he was a battle commander, and, while he padded his figures (as all commanders do), he had to have "an estimate of the situation"; of the population of Mexico he says flatly that Texcoco, one of the largest and most cultivated of the city-states on the mainland facing the city, "must contain some 30,000 inhabitants";

double that sum, be utterly reckless and triple it—Mexico-Tenochtitlán had no more than 90,000 inhabitants. Even "reduced" it was still one of the largest in the world: at that time London had no more than 40,000, Paris could boast 65,000.

Although the Aztec were not an "empire" (as the Inca were an empire), although they had not what most regard as the "essential elements" of civilization—metal, the wheel, dray animals, the rotary quern—they had a form of organization, an intensification of older native techniques, which made possible the achievements that follow and stamped all things they touched indelibly with the word "Mexican."

IV

THE ACHIEVEMENTS

◆◆◆◆◆◆◆◆◆◆◆◆◆◆◆◆◆◆◆◆◆◆◆◆◆◆◆◆◆◆◆◆◆◆◆◆◆◆◆

25. What Mexico Wrought

Aztec architecture perished with the Conquest.

We can mingle our tears with those of Hernán Cortés on that day of Saint Hippolytus, August 13, 1521, when Mexico-Tenochtitlán, in the process of being taken, was utterly destroyed: ". . . one of the most beautiful sights in the world," and with its collapse there was a complete loss of the scale and purpose of its architecture. What was left after the holocaust of conquest were the remains of temples and pyramids adorned with names which jingle like ponderous, brassy tassels and not much more. Nothing has been left of the common houses, not even a ground plan to give an idea of how they were served by their architecture. However, from the existing codices, archaeological excavations, and descriptions by the destroyers, and by means of theoretical reconstruction, we know this: "Public buildings, of a secular character, like the clan or the chief's quarters, were large-scale projections of the domestic architecture." Dr. Vaillant develops this theme: "The addition of many apartments for attendants and concubines, a swimming pool and a menagerie, such as composed the palace of Moctezuma, did not alter structurally or in basic plan the scheme of rectangular rooms set about a patio" —which was the home of the common Indian.

Most of Aztec architecture lay about the immediate vicinity of the lakes, gyrating like satellites around Tenochtitlán. It is all gone. Yet enough has been found in the descriptive literature developed out of archaeology to attempt its reconstruction.

Tenochtitlán appears to have had one of the best planned urban centers of all ancient American cultures. It had not, to be sure, the mechanistic perfection of Cuzco, capital of the Incas, but its attention to human comfort for all the population, its zeal in transporting water through aqueducts, its hedonistic approach to life—often absent in the austere Inca—doubtlessly surpassed all others. The only city-state to which it can be compared, where much of this luxuriousness obtained, was that of Chan-Chan, capital of the Chimor empire in the desert coast of Peru and contemporaneous with the Aztec.

The thought of God is an incitement beyond all else. Religion was the dominating factor in their life and Tenochtitlán was the "city of God"; the whole of it was, in its essence, religious, everything important within it was dedicated, in one form or another, to religion.

The symbol of it was the pyramid. The great *teocalli* stood in the plaza encircled by a high wall fashioned as writhing snakes, and hence its name, *coatepantli*. It measured at its base 150 by 150 feet and rose to about 160 feet high at its truncated apex, which was 70 feet square; on it rested two temples dedicated to the principal gods. While vastly inferior in size to the Temple of the Sun at Teotihuacán or the Temple of Quetzalcoatl at Cholula, it nonetheless was one of the largest and had a great architectural and dramatic effect. It commanded the city, the main road led to it, and it could be seen in the clear atmosphere miles away. The word "pyramid" has unfortunately persisted; these were not pyramids in the Egyptian sense, gargantuan tombs for dead kings catacombed within; they were lofty truncated structures on top of which were the temples, which had a real majesty. "The temple capped the substructure and was the culmination of a harmonious series of ascending planes, calculated to increase the illusion of height by emphasizing the effects of mechanical perspective." [85] The religious, administrative and social aspects of life in the city were grouped, as previously explained, about the temple; this architectural pattern was repeated over and over again, throughout the city. The houses tended to be as squares on a chessboard and formed the basic plan of the rectangular rooms set about a patio.

Water was kept potable by flowing through ceramic pipes and was distributed through the city at fountains where it was gathered in head-balanced water jugs. The small channels were kept open, the larger constantly cleaned; the engineering works and dikes to keep off the rise of lake waters and the long causeways to provide access from the mainland to the island temple-city, the removable bridges and sluice gates, were only part of city planning.

Sanitation was far in advance of anything in Europe until the end of the eighteenth century. So as not to pollute the lake excreta were collected and brought to the mainland fields in canoes, to be used as fertilizer, urine was preserved as a mordant for dying cloth; public latrines were seen by the conquistadors all along the causeways.

All this comes from history; there is little or no physical evidence of it. On the mainland, at Tenayuca, six miles north of Mexico, there are remains of an Aztec temple. It was mentioned during the Conquest, battles in 1520 swirled about it, and the usually informative Bernal Díaz gives no more than its name, calling it the "town of the serpents." Tenayuca was not originally Aztec, having been built between A.D. 1064 and 1116. Mexican archaeologists have found, on excavating, that it had been enlarged six times in its history; the last phase, naturally, was Aztec, and bears that stamp; still their architects did nothing to disturb the chain of serpents which flow open-fanged around three of its sides.[86] What there was of its civic center has completely disappeared.

Tepoztlan, which is fourteen miles northeast of Cuernavaca, has a small temple which crowns the hill overlooking the village of that name. A compact edifice once decorated with sculptured façade, it was not a city, and no other structures remain except a form of triumphant temple erected by Ahuitzotl in 1487, which he dedicated when it came formally within the domains of the Aztec. The temple of Teopanzolco, which also lies on the margin of Cuernavaca, is something like Tenayuca, with its exterior and interior stairway. But there is nothing beyond this. No houses stand here. All that is here is a mute symbol of the power of a militant religion. The essential quality of man, the civic city, the living structure of the house, is missing.

Calixtlahuaca, located near Toluca in the State of Mexico, and within the traditional boundaries of Aztec dominion, is an Aztec structure only by courtesy; it was captured by them in 1476 under the reign of Ahuitzotl and then destroyed by them in 1502. It is so ancient that it has seemingly no precise beginnings; its pottery reveals that the principal temple was begun about A.D. 500.[87] The highest placed site in Mexico, 9,517 feet in altitude, and located in a valley now entirely void of trees, near a large lagoon, it is famous for its Temple of Quetzalcoatl, which is circular, like the convolutions of a seashell, with doors leading into sealed labyrinths within; outside the traditional stairway mounts. The temple was built and rebuilt as tribes invaded the land and with each new conquest left their impress. In all probability it is one of the first such round structures raised in Mexico. Although it was destroyed by the Aztec in 1502, what is interesting is the remains of the *calmecac* portion of the site; these are the

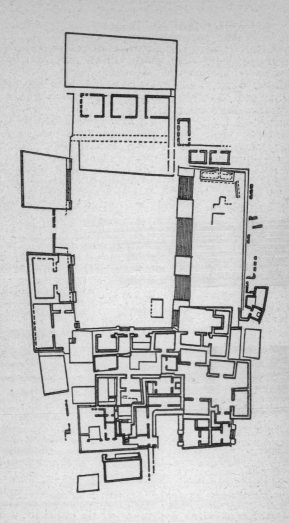

Fig. 41. Calixtlahuaca. The ground plans of an architectural complex, close to the circular temple, known as the house of *calmecac*. The uneven rectangle measure between 125 feet in length by 86 feet in width. Redrawn by Pablo Carrera from a drawing by J. A. Gomez, published by Ignacio Marquina in *Arquitectura Prehispánica*, Mexico, 1951.

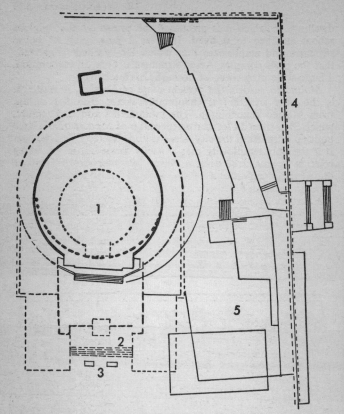

Fig. 42. The circular temple of Calixtlahuaca. Located within
the traditional Aztec territory (near Toluca, State of Mexico), it
is 9,517 feet above sea level, close upon the hill named Tenismo.
The temple is circular (1), and is approached by pyramid steps
(2), in front of which are altars (3). It was surrounded by a
wall (4), and other structures (5), served for the ceremonies
held there. Excavation shows that it had been enlarged many
times. Calixtlahuaca has not been definitely placed in spatial
culture sequence, but since archaic (B.C.), Teotihuacán (A.D.
500), Toltec (A.D. 1000), and Aztec pottery have been found
there, it is presumed that its cultural history covers 2,000 years.
Redrawn by Pablo Carrera from the original plans of Dr. J.
García Payón and published by Ignacio Marquina in *Arquitectura
Prehispánica*, Mexico, 1951.

dwellings in which it is presumed the priests of the religious school attached to it lived. It gives a basic plan of house structure and emphasizes that which Dr. Vaillant suggested: that the most complex Aztec structure is only an elaboration, a large-scale projection, of domestic architecture.

Malinalco, also in the present State of Mexico, is Aztec. It is the only site that is indubitably Aztec that lies distant from Mexico-Tenochtitlán. The monuments and architecture, which date from 1476, during the reign of Moctezuma I, were built 60 miles from the city, close to the village of Tenancingo. It is the only temple-city that is partly hewn out of the living rock. It is not, to be sure, a Petra, "the rose-red city half as old as time" carved out by the Sikh in Transjordania, nor is it as gigantic as the Egyptian rock tombs of Abu Simel, but for America it is unusual enough to border on the unique. *Malinalco,* from *malinalli,* "dry-grass-place," is self-contained, an architecturally composite site of six larger structures and a number of smaller ones. The principal building is hewn round out of the rock ledge, guarded by squatting pumas. At its entrance is a flight of fourteen steps cut out of the living rock. These lead to a temple, whose door once was the open

Fig. 43. Malinalco. A drawing from a wooden drum *(tlapan huehuetl),* showing the spirited dance of the Jaguar and the Eagle. This suggests its dedication to the warrior knights of the Eagle and the Jaguar. Redrawn by Pablo Carrera from a drawing by J. L. Quiroz, published by Ignacio Marquina in *Arquitectura Prehispánica,* Mexico, 1951.

mouth of a fanged snake head. This gives access to a circular chamber where eagles with furled wings and puma heads are carved in the natural rock wall. In another temple there are the remains of an impressive fresco of marching warriors, typically Aztec, with shields and spears "at ready." It is believed by Dr. García Payón, who carried on most of the excavations,[88] that Malinalco was reserved for the rituals of the military orders of the "Eagles" and the "Tigers," the two elite corps of warriors. A beautifully carved wooden drum found at this same Malinalco confirms this theory; around it marches a lively dance of tigers and marching eagles, the symbols of the war cult.

That ends the melancholy parade of what is known of Aztec ruins, places which even in Bernal Díaz's time were razed into nothingness, for he wrote: "Of all these wonders that I then beheld, today all is overthrown and lost, nothing is left standing."

It shows also how utterly incorrect is the term "Aztec empire"; theirs was not, like the Inca's or the Maya's, a homogenous empire, tribe and state; they had domination—not dominion—over the conquered lands held only by troops; there was no political or architectural unity. For instance, the number of Inca structures along the 2,000-mile stretch of their empire is incalculable, there are so many; and the number of temple-cities in the old and new Maya empire reach beyond a hundred; each year sees mor and more sites revealed out of the jungle. Unlike these, the Aztec had no political method of absorbing the conquered populations into their system and imposing upon them an architectural formula. They were essentially a tribute-state. For this reason, to grasp something of Aztec architecture, which had its center in Anáhuac and was destroyed by the Spanish conquest, we must needs go to those from whom the Aztec borrowed and adapted.

Teotihuacán, the temple-city of the Toltec, dwarfs in magnitude all else in Mexico and Middle America. It was in ruins and nameless when the Aztec knew it. Its temple to the Sun, 216 feet high and covering 10 acres of ground, has no peer; all subsequent pyramids, including the Great Teocalli in Mexico-Tenochtitlán, were stylistically based on it. The remains of this great ceremonial city and center, which alone covers an area of eight square miles (and Mexican archaeologists are the first to admit that they have only found a fraction of the whole), date back to as far as 200 B.C. It continued up to 900 A.D. In this vast extent of time the immense temple of the Sun, and its heavenly companion the temple of the Moon, rose to dominate the long avenues of religious structures which are part of Teotihuacán.

The Toltec, famed as architects, craftsmen, knew how to handle mass; their buildings are impressive. The decoration, especially in the well-known temple of Quetzalcoatl, with its great feathered heads as the dominant motif, has a massive awesomeness. Murals uncovered in the temple of agriculture show all the cultivated plants being grown—meaning that every domesticated plant had been developed 1,000 years before the Aztec appeared; the 260-day calendar, great monthly markets, writing, even the familiar Aztec speech-scroll—the human tongue wagging in front of the speaker—had already been perfected long before A.D. 500. All were well-worn cultural elements, taken in the whole or inherited by the Aztec.[89]

Temple-cities are not, to be sure, a pure "American" phenomenon, as V. Gordon Childe explains in his analysis of similar political systems in the Near East; temple-cities functioned in the same way on the Tigris-Euphrates delta, in the Nile Valley and in the Indus Basin around 3000 B.C. They were the logical outcome of an advance in techniques of agriculture, and the harvesting of surplus and improved methods of food conservation transformed luxuries into necessities. As all these types of civilization depended on currying the favor of the gods, the result was the temple-city.

As nearly as 3000 B.C. in Sumer, the temple-city became the repository of social surplus and that surplus produced a new class of people that never existed when society was in the hunting and fishing stage or at the beginning of agriculture—in short, the non-farmer, the specialist, artisans, writers, priests.[90]

Tula, which was such a temple-city 60 miles north of Mexico, is also of Toltec origin and very impressive even in its ruins. It is a mutation of Teotihuacán. Until it was excavated by Mexican archaeologists, its exact place in history could not be gauged; now it is fully obvious that it was the model for the Maya site of Chichén Itzá, 1,000 miles distant in Yucatan. Tula originated new design concepts and new god concepts. The central temple, of greatest interest since the two open-jawed 15-foot-high serpents which served as caryatid-pillars for the temple are the model for a similar structure in Yucatan; the frieze of marching jaguars and high-stepping eagles is repeated in Chichén Itzá (the same motif was used by the Aztec in Malinalco); the carved square pillars of warriors are repeated in the Temple of the Warriors in Yucatan; and the vacant stare of the expressionless and

Fig. 44. Tula. The temple atop the pyramid of legendary Tula or Tollan (A.D. 900–1168), sixty miles north of Mexico City in the modern state of Hidalgo. Tula, belonging to the second phase of the Toltec empire, was a temple-city, and this, the re-constructed main building, was set on top of the truncated pyramid. Redrawn by Pablo Carrera from the water-color of Ignacio Marquina in *Arquitectura Prehispánica*, Mexico, 1951.

terrible figure of Chac-mool, a prone stone figure which holds a depository for freshly torn human hearts, is also repeated by the Aztec and the Maya. All these features had their origin in Tula.

Quetzalcoatl, the culture-hero of this whole land, is closely associated with Tula. He was born on what was to be the most momentous date in Mexico, Ce-acatl, the year of 1-Reed. There was a religious war during his reign, something like the Thirty Years' War in Europe; the city was destroyed and Quetzalcoatl migrated to Cholula on his way to the coast to his "old home in Tlapalan." The glory that was Tula ended with his departure. Civil war worsened with a succession of "kings" and it was finally destroyed about A.D. 1116, and so it disappeared except in tantalizing myth until the Mexican archaeologist Dr. Jiménez Moreno in 1941 began to clean off the detritus of centuries.[91]

Cholula, the city-state of the Mixtec and now the city of Puebla, was the next culture to feel the presence of Quetzalcoatl. Forced to leave Tula, he made his way with a good-sized Toltec force into Cholula; there he stayed and became renowned as a builder of ball courts and the great pyramid which bore his name, so large that the people called it *Tlachi-hual-tepetl,* "Man-made-mountain." This pyramid, torn down by the Spanish to provide building material for Puebla's many churches, was measured by Alexander von Humboldt himself in 1804. He found it to be 187 feet high, its base covering the better part of 44 acres, and it was judged to have been a larger mass than the Egyptian pyramid at Cheops. Its truncated apex, which he sketched, was almost an acre in size; a temple was atop it dedicated to the god of the Air, which was none other than Quetzalcoatl. The Mixtec, very advanced in architectural planning and in the making of pottery and in glyph writing, existed as a tribal entity from 668 A.D. until they were overrun by the Aztec in 1467; their territory spread across the width of Mexico down to the Pacific. When the Spanish arrived there in 1519 they had already been under the domination of the Aztec: "Moctezuma," said Bernal Díaz, "kept many garrisons of warriors stationed in all the provinces"; he had Aztec warriors within and without their capital, Cholula. "The city of Cholula," says Cortés, "is situated on a plain with about 20,000 houses within its walls and as many in the suburbs outside. . . . The city is very fertile (there is not a palm's breadth of land which is not tilled) . . . There is an abundance of land. . . . As for its city . . . its exterior is as fine as any in Spain . . . I . . . counted more than 400 pyramids." [92] Bernal Díaz reports in the same vein: "It is land fruitful in maize, full of magueys from which they make their bever. They make very good pottery . . . supplying Mexico and all the neighbouring provinces. . . . There were many pyramids in the city where the Idols stood, especially the great Cue, Temple of Quetzalcoatl, which was higher than that of Mexico." [93]

Although the Aztec were doubtlessly influenced by Mixtec-Cholula architectural planning, we have been left no details; like the rest it disappeared totally with the Conquest. While here, the Toltec, who were by now reduced to a sort of *condottieri,* made contact with some of the chieftains of Mayapan at the famous trading center of Xicalango, at the edge of Maya territory. There was a civil war in progress in the northern part of Yucatan near Chichén Itzá. The Toltec entered "in A.D. 1194," says the great Maya authority Dr. Morley,[94] and loaded the scales for victory and gained ascendancy over the Maya and at the temple-city of Chichén Itzá at least imposed architectural forms that they brought out of Tula. Whether it was Quetzalcoatl as man that led this Maya invasion, or one bearing this name as a patronymic, his name was imposed again on yet another temple-city. Myth or fact, Quetzalcoatl was to have a fatal effect on the Aztec.[95]

The Aztec, as they conquered, sought new ideas in living and new forms of luxury. They found both in the hotlands of the Gulf Coast. Ahuitzotl during the years 1486-1503 pushed his conquests to northern Vera Cruz, where he encountered the Huastec, who were of Maya speech. There he engulfed one of the oldest cultures, which began about 500 B.C.; he found them very well advanced in town-planning.

The temple-city of Tamuin, close to the river of the same name in the modern state of Tamahuilpas, is especially notable, since its main plaza covered some 20 acres and its temple walls were found to be covered with brilliant frescoes in a style reminiscent of the Toltec. The Totonac were the neighbors of the Huastec. They occupied central Vera Cruz and held dominion over coastal territory close to the Maya. They were, like the others, occupied by the Aztec and tributary to them; they also influenced them in architecture. Moreover, many of their temple-cities are still extant, despite the encroaching jungle.

One of those, Cempoala, is utterly unique. We have a good description of how it appeared to the Spanish in 1519 to compare with the structure as it has grown out of its present-day restoration.

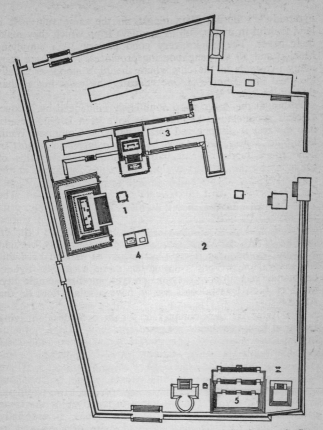

Fig. 45. Cempoala. The walled ceremonial center of Cempoala, in Vera Cruz, built by the Totonacs and occupied by them when the Spaniards began their conquest in 1519. This is the ceremonial center, but the temple-city had a known population of 30,000 living in its environs. The great plaza had an area of 210,000 square meters. The principal temple (1), was seen and commented on by Bernal Díaz del Castillo. The great plaza (2) was walled, which was an unusual architectural feature. The Temple of the Chimneys (3), a rectangular building attached to the main temple, was occupied by priests and chieftains. (4) is a small edifice called the "Altar" and (5) is the great pyramid, explored in the years 1946–47.

In 1519 the Spanish were following the ancient coastal road on the way to Cempoala; they passed, says Cortés, "a few large towns very passably laid out. . . . The houses in those parts which can obtain stone are of rough masonry and mortar, the rooms being low and small, very much after the Moorish fashion. . . . Where no stone can be got they build their houses of baked bricks, covering them over with plaster and a rough kind of thatch. . . . Certain houses belonging to chiefs are quite airy and have a considerable number of rooms . . . we have seen as many as five inner corridors or patios in a single house and its rooms very well laid out around them. Each one of the chief men has in front of the entrance to his house a large patio and some as many as two, three, four, sometimes raised a considerable way off the ground with steps leading up to them and very well built. In addition they have their mosques, temples . . . all of fair size."

Cempoala was 20 miles north from the modern port of Vera Cruz. As they approached it and saw the whitewashed buildings rise out of the green jungle, barbarically colored and vibrant, "we were struck with admiration," said Bernal Díaz, "the streets were so full of men and women who had come to see us—and we reached a great plaza with courts all whitewashed and burnished . . . that one of the scouts thought that this white surface which shone so brightly must be silver."

The whole Totonac land, Cortés estimated, "included as many as 50,000 warriors, 50 villages and strongholds." The Indians were "of middle height, disfigure their faces in various ways, some piercing the ears, introducing large and extremely ugly ornaments . . . others the lower part of nose and upper lip. . . . They wear as clothes a highly coloured poncho, the men wear breech clouts . . . and body cloaks finely worked and painted. . . . The common women wear highly coloured robes reaching from the waist to the feet . . . but the women of high rank wear bodices of fine cotton, very loose fitting, cut and embroidered after the fashion of our bishops and abbots."

When they were at the town itself, Bernal Díaz, talking for everyone, said: "We were struck with admiration. . . . It looked like a garden with luxuriant vegetation and the streets were so full of men and women. . . . We reached a great plaza with courts."

Archaeology has confirmed all that Cortés and his minions said of Cempoala.[96] The temple-city alone with its surrounding houses had a population estimated at about 30,000; the walled plaza—which has been measured and in some parts restored by Mexican archaeologists—had an over-all measurement of 210,000 square meters. The general aspect revealed by research was that it was stone laid with soaring temples. There were fifteen, large and small, within the plaza, the ceremonial center surrounded by one-storied houses, gaily painted and grass-thatched. Dr. J. García Payón, who directed the excavations, found eight large groups of such buildings.

An Aztec garrison was close by. The *pochteca*-merchants made frequent visits and the tribute collectors paid semi-annual calls for tribute. Four of them were there at the time of Cortés's arrival and they were "full of assurance and arrogance," writes Bernal Díaz, "their cloaks and loin-cloths richly embroidered and their shining hair gathered up and tied on their heads." The Aztec thus had access to all this type of town planning and doubtlessly used it. It has been determined that Cempoala was built at the same time as the Aztec sites of Malinalco and Tepoztlan.

North of this city there are remains of other Totonac city-centers. El Tajín, to name but one, 125 miles in a direct line from Vera Cruz and lying 17 miles inland, is a temple-city known since 1785. It has been famous since then for its pyramid of the niches. There are 364 niches representing each day of the long year, which is an unusual architectural feature that somehow has withstood the insults of man and time. Mexican archaeologists have found an immense temple-city surrounding this pyramid, with at least fifteen large structures and numerous smaller ones. Here are all the elements of the "city": pyramid, ball court, raised terraces, palaces. The ball courts are decorated with bas-reliefs, the style of the figures suggesting Mixtec. The subject matter is all the familiar motifs used later by the Aztec; the date 13-Rabbit has been found on one of the stone uprights of the temple of the Columns. One of the favorite sculptural designs used on the buildings is the *xical-coliuhqui*, the-decoration-for-gourds, the most characteristic of Mexican art motifs, derived from the stylized head of the sky-serpent, a symbol of Quetzalcoatl.

In the southern highlands of Mexico there are other cultural centers which influenced Aztec architecture. That which has been the longest known and yet is still the least known is Xochicalco, Place of Flowers, which lies 20 miles south of Cuernavaca. It squats lonely on the highest hills overlooking two fresh-water lakes, two miles distant and in a strongly fortified position. The hills were artificially flattened and terraced, with strong points for defense. Four roads radiate in the four cardinal directions and march up through the impressive buildings into the principal plaza, where the famous temple of Quetzalcoatl stands. Another temple is reached by a ceremonial paved road 60 feet broad.

Xochicalco—its true name is unknown—was a ceremonial and, in addition, perhaps an administrative center; all the familiar edifices are here: palaces, temples, the ball court, and, when finally excavated, there will be found a house-complex within the temple-city—the famous temple to the Plumed Serpent, which has one of the finest façades in all Mexico, has been uncovered. The handling of the figures would suggest Maya were it not for the fire-snakes, which are the symbolism of the Mixtec; the glyphs and dates seem Mixtec and other features suggest Toltec.

Monte Albán lies south of this city in Oaxaca and isolated from the Mexican plateau by a range of mountains sufficiently difficult to prevent an Aztec invasion until 1469.

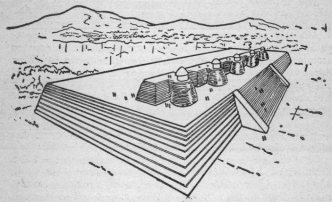

Fig. 46. Plan of the ruins of Tzintzuntzan, located in the present Mexican state of Michoacan, represents a relative rarity. Known in detail only since 1941, Mexican archaeologists found these ruins near the modern village of San Pablo. The ruins, much destroyed by the insults of both time and man, have been reconstructed on what is now known. The platform, called *yacata* and approached by the familiar step pyramid, had on its top a concourse of other pyramidal towers. No spatial cycles have yet been put upon it, but Tzintzuntzan is early. Its pottery—an index of time—points to a time between A.D. 500–800. Redrawn by Pablo Carrera from J. A. Gomez and published by Ignacio Marquina in *Arquitectura Prehispánica*, Mexico, 1951.

A composite of cultures, Olmec, Maya, Zapotec, Mixtec and Aztec, it was perhaps one of the longest continuously inhabited temple-cities known to us (500 B.C.–A.D. 1469). Located on top of the bald hills, 1,500 feet above the level of the valley, although 5,000 feet above the sea, the site has been modified numerous times. When the great Mexican archaeologist Dr. Alfonso Caso first began to excavate it in 1930 and finally concluded the basic part of his work, he found it to be a temple-city set on a large rectangular plaza 2,300 by 820 feet and containing ten large structures: an observatory, a ball court, palaces, and, in the center, a temple-complex with four sets of stairways.

There were five marked periods of occupation: Olmec art adorns the early buildings and this links it to the coastal cultures; there followed a period of Maya influence until the Zapotec exerted their control; this lasted the longest, from A.D. 534 until A.D. 1125. The fourth period found it under the sway of the Mixtec, who brought new art, new gods, a variation in the calendar, tombs, murals, urns; it was they who made the superbly beautiful gold work discovered by Dr. Caso in one of the unopened tombs.[97]

Aldous Huxley, when he visited it, found the site "incomparably magnificent . . . an astonishing situation. . . . Zapotec architects were not embarrassed by the artistic responsibilities imposed upon them . . . they levelled the hilltop . . . laid out the huge rectangular courts. . . . Few architects have had such a sense of austerely dramatic grandeur . . . few have been given so free a hand, religious considerations were never allowed to interfere with the realization of a grand architectural scheme; at Monte Albán they allowed nothing to get in the way of the architects." [98]

The fifth phase of Monte Albán was its last; Moctezuma I surnamed "The Wrathy" set out to conquer Oaxaca in 1469. The Aztec needed it in order to give their merchants passage down to the isthmus of Tehuantepec and so to reach the untouched markets on the western Pacific side of Guatemala and into Central America. They won the temple-city, lost it, and finally, under the next to last leader of the Aztec, captured it and held it until the arrival of the Spanish. It was well known to the Aztec and there is definite evidence that they were influenced by its urban planning.

Mitla, called in the Zapotec language *yoo-paa*, "place of the dead," is part of the same culture; it lies 25 miles directly south of Monte Albán and is not only one of the best-known sites in Mexico but also the best preserved. There are five groups of buildings, extending to both sides of the mostly dry Mitla River. All of them are constructed with the same basic plan which Dr. Vaillant has emphasized characterizes all Mexican structures: rooms formed around a rectangular patio. A cross-section of one of the buildings at Mitla suggests how similar Aztec structures were roofed with giant wooden beams. Architectural façade is unique here, although used by the Maya in Yucatan; the handling of its lines and proportions is unusual. The structures do not stand on pyramids, they are low horizontal masses and have a fortuitous beauty of proportion; there is an austere grandeur in their massive outlines. Aldous Huxley found it "strongly unlike any other, the rooms are decorated with geometrical patterns, all are manifestly inspired by and based on textile designs . . . petrified weaving."

All of these temple-cities, and there are many more, were the source of Aztec architectural ideas and Aztec urban planning. It is a source of regret that so much is gone.

Yet, if the history of Aztec architecture is so fragmentary it is because there was so little.

There was not, architecturally, any such thing as an "Aztec empire."

26. Sculpture

Sculpture was the greatest Aztec contribution to art.

A work of art must be measured by its impact, and if one looks at the powerful and awesome goddess Coatlicue, her head of twin serpents, her necklace of human hands and hearts, her hands claw-armed and her skirt a mass of writhing serpents, it has the same terrible impact the Assyrian bas-reliefs had on one explorer: "My hair alternately stood up and flattened down upon seeing them. . . ."

Much of Aztec sculpture is fearsomely awesome; death was much about them and somehow all this feeling that characterized their sculpture has been hammered into the raw stone. It was this that made a French art historian blanch and turn aside when he saw it: ". . . beautiful, almost always monstrous, contorted, blown up, crushed in, warped . . . one distinguishes nothing but heaps of crushed and palpitating flesh, quivering masses of entrails, a confused pile of viscera."

Realism was the high quality of Aztec sculpture. There were such pieces as that which revolted our Frenchman, but there are others of much delicacy—a rabbit made of white quartz, limpid and pure and very beautiful, a mask formed out of black obsidian, a woman grinding corn, bending over; sculpture had a wide range made to be seen from all sides. It was not like the Maya work, of which Aldous Huxley complained that it was "profoundly, incommensurably alien." Aztec sculpture had an uncanny vitality and unself-consciousness that makes it appeal to the modern eye. As the very observant Pál Kelemen wrote: "The nature of sculpture and the inherent possibilities in the material . . . make it perhaps the most immediately comprehensible of all the arts." [99]

Aztec idols were fearful things to the Spanish; they felt their impact. Thus José de Acosta: "They call this idoll *Tezcallipuca*, he was made of a blacke shining stone [obsidian] like to *iayel*. . . . It had earerings of gold and silver and through the nether lippe a small cannon of crystal. . . ." Yet an Aztec sculptor could handle material ranging from an emerald the size of a pea to immense masses and as large as the great calendar stone, weighing 24 tons. His tools were the simplest: stone celts, awls and drills.

Sculpture was closely linked with architecture. Almost in every structure extant one sees how closely allied were these two functional things: there were sculptured friezes, enormous stone-carved caryatids, columns; sculpture was not a superficial element as is our concept, but a fundamental part of architecture. All of their art was purposeful, functional, and it belonged to religion. *"L'art pour l'art"* had no meaning in Aztec life. Art was purposeful and hieratic; religion was life and life was religion, and sculpture along with all their crafts was tied to it. This is equally true of almost all the art forms of the other tribute-states, Babylonia, Assyria and Egypt.

Aztec sculpture subordinated detail to theme; they had none of that fear of empty space which caused the Maya to overcrowd design with detail; their aim was impact. The stone piece of the goddess Xipé has the flayed god appearing so simply quaint, it was as if the sculptor's small daughter had been the model, until, looking at the back, one becomes aware that Xipé is attired in a freshly flayed skin of a sacrificial victim.

Different from all these and buried in a mass of ritualistic detail is the Aztec calendar stone. Two years in the carving (1479–81), it stood 12 feet high and weighed 24 tons. It embodies "a finite statement of the infinity of the Aztec universe," with the face of the Sun god Tonatiuh in the center and twenty names of days circling it; it is filled with symbols of previous world epochs, symbols of heaven and color; a grandiose conception of the universe.

Aztec sculpture is a quality. One does not have to be versed in all the intricacies of religious symbolism to enjoy it. Pál Kelemen wrote that it could be enjoyed as pure sculpture detached from any precise culture.

27. The Lapidaries
Goldsmiths and Jewel-Carvers

Metalwork came late to Mexico. It came up by slow degrees from South America.

None of the early cultures worked metal; it does not appear at Teotihuacán, which was already a memory when the technique of gold and copper working reached Mexico. It was unknown to the early Maya and the Olmec craftsman contented himself with making diadems of jade. It was not perfected in Mexico much before the eleventh century.

Gold makes life sumptuous; the Aztec knew it and traded for it. As Bernal Díaz saw it, it was free to be traded in the market places: "placed in thin quills of geese, so that the gold could be seen through it."

Mining was rudimentary. Gold was panned or collected in nuggets; silver, which seldom occurs pure in nature, was more of a problem and was less used. Gold is a metal of great ductility, for a single grain can be drawn into a wire 500 feet long; it was worked by the Aztec with the simplest of techniques. It was melted in a furnace heated by charcoal, draught being supplied by a man blowing through a tube into the charcoal embers. There are few implements extant but we have been left illustrations of goldsmithery. They worked the gold by means of hammering, embossing, plating, gilding, sheathing. Out of this simple, almost crude, technique came gold pieces which excited more than the cupidity of the conquistador. There were "three blow guns" said Bernal Díaz, "with their pellet molds and their coverings of jewels and pearls, and pictures of little birds covered with pearl shell."

Most of the gold extracted from Moctezuma, some 600,000 pesos weight of it, was melted down into ingots; some of it

153

they thought too beautiful to destroy, like the pieces they received at Vera Cruz at the beginning of the adventure: "A wheel like a sun, as big as a cartwheel with many sorts of pictures on it . . . and a wonderful thing to behold . . . then another wheel of greater size . . . of silver of great brilliance in imitation of the moon. Then they brought 20 golden ducks, beautifully worked and very natural looking and some ornaments like dogs, others shaped like tigers, lions, monkeys, 12 arrows and a bow with a golden string . . . all in beautiful hollow work of gold." All this was sent intact to Carlos V. He being then in Flanders, Cortés's ship was sent after him. He was at last found in Brussels, and, on July 12, 1520, Cortés's ambassadors presented the Aztec gold work to him. His comment, whatever it was, has not been recorded. That gold, like all the rest that came from the Americas, went into his crucibles to be made into ingots to pay the soldiery to maintain him on the nebulous throne of the Holy Roman Empire. Fortunately the great Albrecht Dürer was there at the same time and he left his impressions of it in his diary. Himself a descendant of a line of Hungarian goldsmiths settled in Nuremberg, and knowing what he was seeing, Dürer wrote:

I saw the things which were brought to the King [Carlos V] from the New Golden Land [Mexico]; a sun entirely of gold, a whole fathom broad; likewise a moon entirely of silver, just as big; likewise sundry curiosities from their weapons, arms and missiles . . . all of which is fairer to see than marvels. . . .

These things were all so precious that they were valued at 100,000 gulden. But I have never seen in all my days what so rejoiced my heart as these things. For I saw among them amazing artistic objects and I marvelled over the subtle ingenuity of the men in these distant lands. Indeed I cannot say enough about the things which were there before me.

That was the only commentary by anyone whose opinion meant anything in these things. Carlos V ordered that henceforth all gold and silver coming from the Indies be melted down on arrival. Little survived. Only the wonderful descriptions of the conquistadors, which, since there was no gold later to be found or seen, historians of the eighteenth century took as the natural braggadocio of such men. It was only when Dr. Alfonso Caso found the undisturbed tomb of a Mexican chieftain at Monte Albán in 1931 and the superbly beautiful necklaces, earplugs, and rings, that historians realized that the simple honest Bernal Díaz was making a magnificent understatement.

Goldsmiths had a guild. Those attached to Moctezuma's many-roomed household were non-taxpayers; they were supplied with placer gold and busied themselves making pieces for Moctezuma and other officials. Bernal Díaz speaks of the "workers in gold and silver, and of these there were a great number in the town of Atzcapotzalco, a league from Mexico." As the gold was sold in the market, presumably any craftsman who had enough to barter for the goose quills of gold dust could work it up in jewelry for himself or else for trade.

Lapidaries, workers in precious stones, were many, and, like the others: "skilled workmen which Moctezuma employed." Foremost of the stones was jade. This was found in southern Mexico and Guatemala and valued more than gold itself, which Bernal Díaz found to his satisfaction, for he took four jades during the first Spanish retreat from Tenochtitlán and they "served me well in healing my wounds and gathering me food."

Jade was an article of tribute and the glyph for it is found in the Book of Tributes. Now there is a difference, mineralogically, between the jade of America and the Oriental, and that should put to rest the idea that the American Indian got his jade from China; it is "American." It is utterly amazing how the Aztec craftsman achieved the delicate handling of so hard a stone; it required great patience. Everything of jade was saved, even the smallest pieces of the "precious green," to be put in the mouths of the dead, to take the place of the stilled heart.

Masks were often made of jade, or, when it was not available, of less valued green stone. Masks, with their expressionless slit eyes and swollen lips, were a feature among all of these cultures. Some are exquisite, others are repetitious and "vulgar," as the astute Pál Kelemen noted. These powerful artistic impulses "were stereotyped through constant repetition." The truth is that most art has always been either bad or indifferent, as Aldous Huxley said when looking at the same thing: "Vulgarity is always the result of some excess; vulgarity is an inward tendency toward the excessive." This holds for any who dominated: "Vulgarity has always been the privilege of the prosperous."

The skill among the lapidaries was broad; the large objects doubtlessly were done by the "professionals," yet much was done by the ordinary craftsman. Crystal, a very hard stone, is not easily worked, yet the Aztec shaped art forms out of it from the smallest of pieces to the life-size crystal skull. This latter symbiosis of beauty and death sits, divorced from its conception, before black velvet curtains in the British Museum.

Turquoise came by trade from the north. It was much in demand and traveled almost as far to Mexico and Yucatan as did amber (that "special act of God") in the Old World. The Aztec exacted turquoise as a form of tribute and it so appears from eleven towns on the tribute-rolls; it was used with other materials for the making of mosaics on masks, knives and even walls.

Obsidian glass (*itzli*) was an Aztec specialty; it was exported as raw material and as finished product. Found close by, a product of volcanic action, obsidian was used for knives, razors, lip-plugs, mirrors of high polish, and other objects of immense beauty.

Emeralds (*quetzal-itzli*) were the excitement, as much for the Aztec as for the Spanish: "The Kings of Mexico didde much esteeme theme; some did use to pierce their nostrils and hang them therein," says José de Acosta, "on the visages of their idolles." As soon as Moctezuma was elected as chief speaker, the first thing he did was "to pierce the gristle of his nostrils, hanging thereat a rich emerald."

The conquistador saw them as a symbol of riches; Hernán Cortés commandeered the whole of them for himself; he knew that Cleopatra wore emeralds and that a Christian pilgrim lately from India saw them in a temple of Buddha, "flashing their fire 200 leagues on a cloudless night." As for the source, Moctezuma expressed ignorance; they were from "the south." In fact, they were from only one region, the mountain areas in Colombia, about Muzo, which was the only source of emeralds at that time. They were plenteous in Colombia, where they were used for barter to obtain cotton and gold dust. They were well-known in Panama and used to great effect in combination with gold. They were obtained for Moctezuma by the activities of his *pochteca*-merchants who penetrated beyond Nicaragua. Emeralds are soft and chip easily, yet the Aztec cut them in intricate patterns, flowers, fish, fanciful forms of exquisite workmanship. Hernán Cortés got his emeralds directly from Moctezuma, one in a pyramidal shape, "broad as the base of the hand," others so fabulous that Carlos V is said to have coveted the fantastic baubles. Cortés refused 400,000 ducats in Genoa for them, saving them for Doña Juana de Zúñiga, his betrothed, a daughter of a ducal family. He gave her five Aztec-worked emeralds, "one in the form of a rose, one like a bell with a pearl for a tongue, one like a fish, one like a trumpet, one like a cup." [100]

28. Feather Weaving

The feather weaving on mosaic was another of the Aztec accomplishments. Examples of it have disappeared completely because of conquest and climate. The only examples of real magnificence of this art are preserved by mere accident of history. The rest has perished. Similar feather weavings found in the desert coast of Peru and well preserved despite the passage of time have given us an idea of the technique; we also have illustrations of artisans weaving feathers in the work of Bernardino de Sahagun.

Feather weavers (*amanteca*) were highly appreciated; they formed a guild and were of the professional class. In feather weaving, quills were inserted into the web, each quill was hooked over a thread and secured by a knot in the second row, leaving only the color part of the feather visible on the other side. As is obvious, the color pattern had to be carefully arranged as a mosaic before the feathers were applied. Shields, headgear, cloaks, banners, totem emblems, were all done in feather weaving. Warriors so accoutered die beautifully.

Since colorful birds were limited in the altitudes of Mexico-Tenochtitlán, there was much activity on the part of the merchants to obtain bird feathers when the local supply did not meet the demand.

Birds of all climes were brought alive to Mexico and their habitats simulated; the waterfowl alone had separate pools, as attested by Hernán Cortés: "ten pools of water in which were kept every kind of waterfowl known." There was no such thing in Europe until Padua in 1545 erected a zoological garden. The type of food and water depended on the bird. There were three hundred men employed to look after them and "each pool was overhung by balconies cunningly arranged from which Moctezuma would delight to watch the birds." [101] In another part were cages for the land birds, wooden trellises cleverly made, 9 feet high and 18 feet around; there were another three hundred men to look after these. Bernal Díaz could not even name all of the various species that he saw in that aviary: "birds of great size, down to tiny birds of many-coloured plumage." The birds bred in the cages, too. As they molted the feathers were gathered, selected, graded and brought to the feather weavers.

Let no one doubt the magnificence of this art. One piece has been preserved, the headdress sent by Moctezuma to Hernán Cortés when he first landed at Vera Cruz, and was believed to be Quetzalcoatl returning to reclaim his empire. This was sent in turn to Carlos V who passed it on to his fellow Habsburg, Archduke Ferdinand of Tyrol; it was long preserved in the castle at Ambras. When discovered and its history made known, it was sent to Vienna, and there today it rests in a burst of golden-green iridescence in the Museum für Völkerkunde; a double assurance, if that be needed, of the sense of beauty of the Aztec.

Everyone in Aztec society was some sort of craftsman. "Art" as a name for this is in all probability not the right word for these productions, yet is there another? The Aztec was a maker of things; everything was functional, real, purposeful. As Aldous Huxley pointed out when he examined all this for the first time: "craft culture brought psychological fulfilment . . . a society of craftsmen was a society of satisfied individuals, more, it had a human wholeness. A primitive is forced to be whole, a complete man, able to fend for himself in all circumstances, if he is not whole, he perishes." But was the Aztec impressed by his craftmanship, his "art"? Dr. Vaillant thought not: "They did not speculate about aesthetics." Yet a Mexican sociologist, going through Nahuatl texts,[102] believes they did and that they were animated by a real sense of beauty. He has translated the "song of the painter":

The good painter, understanding god in his heart,
defines things with his heart, dialogues with his own heart.

The Nahuatl texts now made available to us [103] show many expressions that suggest this attitude was not an isolated instance. In the presence of his "art" the craftsman felt the "divinity of things." For listen to the song, well-remembered and sung over and over again to later generations, of a birdkeeper who saw death fall upon Mexico-Tenochtitlán and destruction of the aviaries which he cared for all perish in the flames:

> the plumes of the quetzal
>> the works of iridescent jade
>> all broken and gone
>> the memory of a beautiful world,
>>> god-filled, truth-filled . . .

If then, this real feeling is true, how explain the other world of the Aztec, the "apparent incongruity" as Prescott wrote, "of a comparatively refined people of often gentle influences whose religion was of a spirit of unmitigated ferocity." Why did the Aztec inhale the perfume of corpses as if it were some aphrodisiacal perfume?

29. Religion, War and Administration

War and religion, at least to the Aztec, were inseparable. They belonged to each other. "It is no exaggeration to say," observes a recent writer on the subject,[104] "that the government of [Aztec] Mexico was organized from top to bottom so as to be able to sustain, and thereby mollify, the unseen powers with as many human hearts as it was possible to give them."

Blood was the drink of the gods. To obtain appropriate prisoner-victims as sacrifice for the gods, there were ceaseless little wars, for one could hardly expect the Aztec to offer themselves in endless lines for immolation. At the outset it would serve little to explain this attitude in moral terms. All militant religions have been involved in bloodletting in one form or another.

The object of Aztec religion was to attract favorable forces to it and repulse or at least mollify those which were not. They knew that nature moved in a series of rhythmic patterns. They put all their observatory powers to work to "discover what these rhythms were" and to harness them, not alone for their own good but for all mankind's survival. "From this point of view," wrote Dr. Alfonso Caso, "magic and science are alike: both are techniques which aim at the control of the world and both consider that magic or nature are a necessary link between phenomena." [105]

Since man always turns things into an image of himself, it would have been impossible for the Aztec to have a mental image that was not anthropomorphic, so natural forces among them were personified. As the society grew complex, the gods grew in complexity and they took on specialized functions.

In the forefront of the Aztec pantheon was a sun-god

who brought life by his daily appearance; sun-worship was an essential part of Aztec religion. There were the gods of the four cardinal directions, each symbolized by his own color, "since," as Dr. Vaillant wrote, "the Aztec universe was conceived on a religious rather than a geographic sense." Gods were appointed, with their colors, in keeping with the preconceived prejudices of their own life history: east was red; south was blue, and evil; west was white (it had good auguries); north was black, a pallor of gloom and presided over by Mictla-tecuhtli, Lord of the Dead.

There were personal gods, each plant had its god, each function its god or goddess, even suicides had one. Yacatecuhtli was the deity of the merchants. In this polytheistic world all gods had clearly defined traits and functions. So the pantheon grew more complex as the people took to worshiping the different manifestations of the gods and this duality made the pantheon so bewildering that only the priests, whose function it was, could keep track of them all.

The Aztec gods warred in Aeschylean grandeur. The gods of evil—for the Aztecs believed in immanent evil as do those of the Jamesian school of literature—fought with the beneficent gods. Light and darkness struggled for man's soul.

Yet all this was beyond the pale of mere man. He kept to the little gods. The image of the corn-goddess he purchased at the market—a stamped clay figure which he buried in his *milpa*-field with prayers and tears. There were household gods set up in some remote corner. There was the goddess of the maguey, Mayahuel, whose spirit was evoked when they drew the sweet syrup and converted it into an intoxicant.

All these earth-gods were their life. The complicated religious pattern they left to the priests, who told them when to weep, when to get drunk, when to rejoice, when to die. The people seemed content to resign themselves to those who spoke of the unknowable with so great a certainty.

Huitzilopochtli, the Hummingbird Wizard, was the Aztec's own. They were his children, the "chosen people." He it was who led them out of the dry misery of the north into the promised land of Mexico-Tenochtitlán; he took his place among all the other gods, from the ancient past and from other cultures. He was the sun, the ever youthful warrior who fought battles with the other gods for man's survival. Each day he rose, fought the night, the stars, the moon, and, armed with sun-bolts, brought on the new day. Since he fought these battles for them the Aztec could only repay by nourishing him for his eternal wars. The proffered food could be none of this watered-down intoxicant pulque, nor corncakes such as mortal man ate—the god must be nourished on the stuff of life: blood. It was the sacred duty of every Aztec—for all were part of an agrarian militia—to take prisoners for sacrifice in order to obtain human hearts and blood—the nectar of the gods for Huitzilopochtli.

War, eternal war, then, was bound up with religion. How else could human hearts be obtained? A long peace was dangerous, and war thus became the natural condition of the Aztec for if the beneficent gods were not nourished they would cease to protect man from the other gods and this might lead to the total destruction of the world. When the great temple-pyramid to Huitzilopochtli was dedicated in Mexico in 1486, "king" Ahuitzotl, after a two-years' war campaign in Oaxaca, amassed more than 20,000 prisoner-victims. These were lined up in rows waiting to be spread-eagled over the sacrificial stone. Their hearts were cut out and held briefly to the sun, then, still pulsating, deposited in the heart-urn of the recumbent Chac-mool figure.

The ritual for all this became as complex as that which now surrounds that religion which Norman Douglas called that "quaint Alexandrian tutti-frutti known as Christianity."

The priests directed the intellectual and religious life of Mexico. At the top of the pinnacle was the Chief Speaker— "the king," to the Spanish. He was more than an ex-officio high priest; his was the final tribunal.

Two high priests (*quequetzalcoa*) were resident in Mexico. Under them was another who administered the business end of tribute-tithes and who supervised the schooling of new priests (*tlamacazqui*) and the establishment of the faith in the newly conquered villages. There were, it is said, 5,000 attached to the temples in Mexico-Tenochtitlán alone. They dressed in black, their *tilmantli* was ornamented with a border of skulls and entrails. Bernal Díaz said that the priests had "long robes of black cloth like those of the Dominicans . . . their hair was very long and so matted with blood that it could not be separated or disentangled."

They elaborated cult rituals, taught in the religious schools, helped train those who traced out the rituals, worked with the *tlacuilo*-artists, taught and extended the knowledge of hieroglyphic writing and the symbols of the complicated mathematical and astronomical computations. They helped the architects to delineate the temples and buildings, and when finished arranged the ritual of sacrificial dedication. They helped to create music and dances, arrayed them, prescribed the things to hear, proscribed those not to be heard. They intervened with the unseen powers, remembered and chanted the historical events until they became fixed in human memory. This theocracy pervaded everything in Aztec life.

"The gods ruled," wrote Dr. Vaillant, "the priests interpreted and interposed and the people obeyed."

30. The Calendar

The calendar was at the base of every action of the Aztec. There were two calendars, the ritualistic one *(tonalpohualli,)* * a parade of 260 days; and a second which was a genuine solar calendar of the conventional length year of eighteen 20-day months; a lunar reckoning of 360 days plus five uncounted days, the empty *nemontemi*.

The first was magical and sacred; it bore little relation to astronomical observation, and the origin of the cycle has never been satisfactorily explained. It was very ancient; the Aztec gave it nothing, for it had been known to the Maya under the name of *tzolkin* for 1,500 years. The divinatory cycle consisted of twenty periods of thirteen days and each of these twenty periods of thirteen had a name—*calli* (house), *coatl* (snake), *malinalli* (grass), *tochtli* (rabbit, etc.—and each of the thirteen days a number. Thus the days of the month would read 1-rabbit, 2-rabbit, etc., until the next "month" began. This recurring again and again in a continuous 52-year cycle, or 18,980-day period, was such that no day could be confused with another, since the name of the month and its associated number precluded any repetition in this cycle.

The solar "year-bundle" *(xiuhmolpilli)*, as the Aztec called it, consisted of 365 days, divided into eighteen months of twenty days each. The remaining five, "the empty days" *(nemontemi)*, were the unlucky days and neither named nor counted, just as in New York City many buildings do not have a thirteenth floor. Now the least common multiple of 20 on 13 and 365 (whose primes are 5 and 73), as Franz Boas graphically explained,[106] is 52 x 365 or 18,980 days. This was the 52-year cycle; after this period the same divinatory combination repeated itself. In another form the Aztec astronomer-mathematicians, or those from whom they obtained this most com-

* This is often mistakenly called the *tonalamatl;* this referred to the physical book in which the *tonalpohualli* was recorded.

Miguiztli	Mazatl	Tochtli	Atl
Itzcuintli	Ozomatli	Malinalli	Acatl
Ocelot	Cuauhtli	Cozcaquauhtli	Ollin
Tecpatl	Quiauitl	Xochitl	Cipactli
Ehecatl	Calli	Cuetzpallin	Coatl

Fig. 47. Aztec day signs. A solar calendar was divided into eighteen 20-day months (with five empty days); the sacred calendar was divided into twenty 13-day months. The day signs were used in both calendars.

plicated ingenious calendar, determined that the two calendars, divine and solar, also gave the combination of 20 x 13 x 73 which resulted in the same 18,980 days, making again the magical 52-year cycle.

Why this 52-year cycle? Why was fleeting time so great an obsession with the Aztecs? Why did it become a national fetish so that they really believed that at the end of a 52-year cycle the very future of the world was in balance and might be destroyed? Did the very cleverness of the mathematicians seduce them? Did the fact that these two calendars just happened to coalesce in the various calculations to make the 52-year cycle seem so magical that they conceived their inventions to be really a basic fact of nature?

No one knows. The shock of discovery must have been as profound to them as M. Jourdain's discovery in Molière's *Le Bourgeois Gentilhomme* that he had been speaking prose all his life.

The Aztec's relation with time was fundamentally emotional. Then priest-astronomers had put great intellectual effort into the elaboration of the calendar. As calendar, it was more advanced than in either Egypt or Greece. Egypt and Mesopotamia had lunar calendars, i.e., the beginning of every new month was determined by the waxing or waning of the moon. They made up for the discrepancy between lunar and solar by having "hollow" and "full" months, and this crude form of calendar existed down to Roman times. All peoples strongly agricultural in character gave great importance to the solar year, but the cities in the "fertile crescent" had different calculations, which produced chaos in comparative time reckoning. Egypt (as did the Maya and Aztec) had two systems: a religious lunar calendar, a civil 365-day calendar, and a 25-year cycle.

The Greeks in the time of Hipparchus (150 B.C.), taking over the whole of Babylonian science, began to use "the methods of computing sexagesimally and the place-value notation, including a symbol for zero," [107] but the use of the zero-symbol never came into general practice until the Hindus perfected it in the eighth century A.D. Yet the "American" cultures were far, far in advance of all this; the Maya invented zero and could calculate their day count as far into the past as 1,152,000,000 days.[108]

Why all this? Why this extraordinary preoccupation with time? Did they find the endless continuity of time so appalling even though they marked it into spatialized periods with rituals and festivals? No one knows. The dominant note was the 52-year cycle; the whole of the tribe's intellectual forces were put to work long before its advent to allay the wrath of the gods.

The priests had to calculate ritual by most involved methods, they had to know the precise interconnection between each particular god and "time" as given on the calendar. Sacrifice had to be correctly calculated so that it would benefit the particular god to whom they were appealing. All the developed intellect of the Aztec was turned toward this one thing: how to propitiate the right god at the right time. So sacrifice was not mere butchery, it was a parade of elaborately conceived ritual with only one object in view: to preserve human existence.

For the Aztec was threatened not only at the end of each 52-year cycle; when the priests announced the end of each year there came the dreaded *nemontemi*, the "five empty days." Fires were extinguished, fasting was general, sexual intercourse ceased; artists left off their work, business lay untransacted. The same thing occurs in the Austrian Tyrol when the *Föhn*—the warm south wind—blows: important business grinds to a halt. No transaction on these days had legality. On that dawn of the fifth day, when the priest-astronomers, consulting their calendar books, observed the Pleiades rising in the heavens and knew the world would not end, they reached out and found a sacrificial victim, slashed open his chest, pulled out his heart, and in the freshly weeping wound kindled a new fire; from it all the fires in the temples were rekindled and from it people all over Mexico-Tenochtitlán gathered the new fire for the new year. All was right once more with the Aztec world.

31. War

War was the errant of this religion.

It was, as is seen, related directly to religion (captives for sacrifice). It was related to economy (supplying tribute for the tribute-state). War was an Aztec preoccupation; it was sacred, it had a mystic-religious quality which made it all the more ferocious. Every able-bodied man was a warrior, part of an agrarian militia; the only professional army in the Aztec confederation was the small coterie of well-born warriors who formed the bodyguard of the "First Speaker." The Aztec had universal service hundreds of years before Napoleon returned to nature by using the onset of a mass army without regard to losses (instead of the artificial maneuvers with small bodies of troops favored in Baroque times). The Aztec warrior was hard and spartan; he was trained to be so since childhood. His land was not lush, life was not easy, he was given only one choice, victory or death by sacrifice. Life, if it would be great, the Aztec attitude emphasized, is hard, and to victory belongs the sacrifice of victory.

War is the primary of politics. It was to the Aztec then; it is the same to us, the living. Politics is the way in which a fluent being maintains itself and the character of war and politics is quite the same: [109] tactics, stratagems, material forces applied at the moment of truth are the same in both, ". . . the growth of one's own way of life at the expense of the other."

War as a branch of politics began with the powwow. Ambassadors, called *quauhquauh nochtzin*, were sent to the village or tribe under pressure to join the Aztec "commonwealth"; trade and road protection were offered. With the compact came the demand that the Aztec national god Huitzilopochtli be placed by (but not replace) their local deity. They were to be allowed to keep their own dress, manners and chieftains; they would yield tribute every six months. Negotiations were long and involved;[110] they were given the length of a lunar calendar month to capitulate.

When war was decided in council, the leaders gathered in front of the stone of Tizoc in the great plaza. Set up during the reign of Tizoc (1481–86), the large cylindrical block of trachyte, 8 feet in diameter and carved with figures in low relief, shows Aztec warriors capturing others in battle, which is symbolized by the warrior grasping a lock of the enemy's hair.[111] It was set up facing the great *teocalli*-temple; there or near to it the final act of war was got in motion.

The war lord held office only for the duration of a particular campaign. He was generally related by blood ties to the "First Speaker." His war dress was elaborate; there are murals still extant that show him accoutered in quetzal feathers, ofttimes with a fantastic headgear. It was impossible not to discern him in battle and one of the prime objects was his capture. The elite of battle, the military order of the Eagle, wore a mimicry of an open eagle's beak and feather weavings of eagle feathers; the military order of the Jaguar dressed

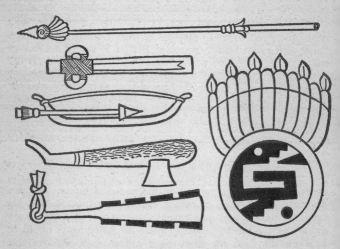

Fig. 48. Aztec weapons. The round object was a shield (*chimalli*) which bore the crest of the clan. The most-feared weapon was the *maquahuitl*, the sword toothed with obsidian blades. The bow was a Toltec weapon, used by the Aztec and introduced into Maya country in the tenth century. The javelin (*mitl*) was thrown with the aid of a spear-thrower, and had great force.

in jaguar skins; the soldiers, other common warriors from the clans, wore distinct tunics. Their shields also had a totemic device of their clan. Before they set off, priests had to consult the *tonalamatl*-horoscope to divine if the moment was propitious for victory. And why not? The Inca consulted the lungs of sacrificed llamas to see if the auguries were right, the Romans consulted chicken livers; the Aztec, consulting the stars in their orbit, were at least a bit more saturated with reason. If observations suggested dubious victory they did not enter into war until later.

The Aztec, in comparison with the European standards of 1519, were lightly armed; headgear when worn was more decorative than protective; they did, however, wear quilted cotton tunics, soaked in brine; as Bernal Díaz observed, they "wore armour made of cotton reaching to the knees." For the hot country it was superior to Spanish armor. All carried shields (*chimalli*) to deflect arrow or sword cut; these were made of wood covered with animal hide; many were extremely decorative, with the totemic device of the clan. The closing-in weapon was the *maquahuitl;* it was of hardwood edged with blades of obsidian sharp enough for a warrior to sever a horse's head. The bow (*tlauitolli*), with obsidian-tipped arrows, they used with deadly effectiveness "and with great skill," confesses Bernal Díaz, who received many in his own hide in his time; "the first flight of arrows wounded fifteen soldiers." In addition to these they had the sling, which hurled an egg-sized stone, and, most effective, the obsidian-tipped javelin (*mitl*), which was thrown with great force by means of the *atl-atl* spear thrower. Bernal Díaz remembered that in one of their battles on the coast, the Indians "let fly such a cloud of javelins . . . that they wounded seventy of us."

The nature of the land conditioned Aztec strategy. Wars had to be of short duration. They had no beasts of burden, everything had to be carried on the backs of human carriers. There was no system of supply such as the Inca in Peru set up along finely developed roads; siege wars under these conditions were almost impossible since no Aztec army could be kept on the field for more than a few days. Besides, the Aztec plan was not to slaughter unnecessarily or destroy; death and destruction would imperil tribute, which was the primary aim of the battle, along with the need for sacrificial victims.

In general there were no walled cities, although the Maya had one at Tulum in Yucatan and the hereditary enemies of the Aztec, the Tlascala, built a wall 15 feet high surrounding their large towns.*

The watery defense of Mexico-Tenochtitlán was a deterrent to any save the Spanish and in general there were no fortifications. Fighting was in the open. There were no "secret weapons," all had the same type of arms; what counted most in battle was surprise, ambush, morale. Battle began with a war of nerves: there were military promenades to overawe the enemy, warriors came with drums, conch-shell horns (the type seen in the Maya murals at Bonampak). The Spaniards in their first encounter got the same treatment; the Indians were "drawn up in battle array whistling and sounding their trumpets and drums."

Before the campaign got under way, ambassadors had to be sent to towns and villages, subject or not, for them to arrange supplies. It was almost impossible to hide intent in a major undertaking. In some instances the Aztec deliberately refrained from use of surprise, not only giving their enemy time to arm, but sometimes even sending them arms, to develop the premise that the outcome on the battlefield was, in truth, the will of the gods.

When at a distance of an arrow flight from each other, the opposing warriors released their shafts over the heads of their forward forces; then they hurled rocks, accurately enough, from plaited cotton slings. Spears followed, which really wrought havoc; then in a welter of noise and fearful shouting they fell on each other with the *maquahuitl*, the closing-in weapon. The object was to capture the leader. Often this alone was enough to decide the issue—a single battle could suffice; again enmities could be protracted over the years. Slaughter was only to cause a rout, when that happened they took prisoners. The retreat was followed up by the Aztec into the principal tribal city; usually the priests with some warriors put up a determined resistance on the steps of their sacred *teocalli*-temple. In token of victory the Aztec burned the temple, for that is the symbol of conquest in their glyph writing. Peace was arranged as quickly as possible and normality restored. Then the tribute-tribunal fixed the amount and kind to be yielded every six months. The warrior-prisoners were sent to Tenochtitlán to be held for sacrifice; if the tribe was unreliable, an Aztec garrison was placed close by and their chieftains were sent as hostages to the Aztec capital. No attempt was made at absorption of

* A part of this defense wall can still be seen at Huexotla (State of Mexico).

the newly conquered into Tenochtitlán. "The idea of absorbing conquered towns into the victorious state . . . never occurred to the Mexican," says Dr. George Vaillant, "and even defeated towns retained their local autonomy." There were revolts, naturally, and the Aztec militia had to be kept constantly on the go; this one defect in their political system was their Achilles' heel.

There never was an Aztec empire. They were never able somehow to transform domination into dominion.

32. The Tribute State

The Aztec state was a tribute state.

Although trade was vast, extending down to Nicaragua and perhaps beyond, although things Mexican traveled as far north as Arizona for an interchange of products (Moctezuma was said to have had a bison in his zoological gardens); although the Aztec people were good craftsmen and produced for "export"—still the state in its later development depended on tribute exacted from conquest. The Aztec knew, without the benefit of an Oswald Spengler, that "war is the creator and hunger the destroyer of all great things" and that whole peoples have lost force through the gnawing wretchedness of living. When an Aztec warrior died, he died *for* something, not *of* something. Total war was not part of their policy, nor did they want to liquidate or force the erstwhile enemy into abject poverty; they wanted tribute.

This imperial appetite began after 1400 A.D. It continued under the various "kings" until by 1519 the Aztec dominated —with tribute yield—those parts of Mexico beginning in the north about Tampico across to Lake Chapala, thence southward including almost all of the southern part of Mexico up to the domain of the Maya. It was large enough to include 371 tribute towns and sufficiently complex that they had to keep tribute rolls so extended that Hernán Cortés had to admit to his King-Emperor: "I was unable to find out exactly the extent of Moctezuma's kingdom. . . . The king has fortresses in all those provinces armed with his own men and also overseers and tax-collectors." And: "the tribute is inscribed in written characters and pictures." These were the tribute rolls (or, since they were folded screen-wise—books), the same that Bernal Díaz saw at Tenochtitlán: "A great Cacique . . . kept the accounts of the revenue that was brought to Moctezuma in his books, which were made of *amatl*-paper . . . and he had a great house full of them."

Fig. 49. The collecting of tribute was done every six months. Various objects of tribute collected from conquered tribes or those living under Aztec hegemony are seen here. There is a shield, blankets, *huipillis*; in another section Indians bring in corn and squash. One of the tribute collectors studies the tribute charts.

A copy of one of these is still extant, with names, products and amounts from tribute towns. Antonio de Mendoza, the first Viceroy to Mexico (1535–50), had one of these tribute charts copied. It was drawn by a native artist, the glyphs translated and written in parallel Spanish orthography. It was intended as a gift to Carlos V; instead French pirates seized the Spain-bound vessel at Vera Cruz and by a chain of events too complicated to follow it came to rest in the hands of André Thévet, the famous cosmographer to the king of France. He sold it for twenty crowns in 1584 to the English traveler and publisher of discoveries, Richard Hakluyt; it was translated with the idea that Sir Walter Raleigh would publish it at his expense, but he left his head in the Tower before this could be accomplished. It then came into the hands of Samuel Purchas, the clerical publisher of travel literature, and so it first appeared in *Purchas his Pilgrimes* in 1625. After being "lost" for two centuries in the Biblioteca Bodleiana at Oxford, the *Codice Mendocino* (named after the one who had had it made), was included, in 1831, in the aforementioned *Antiquities of Mexico*.

Tribute covered every phase of Aztec wants and Aztec luxuries. Foremost were various elaborate war costumes: helmets, shields, jaguar skins for warriors of that order, eagle skins for the other; clothing included all that man wore in Mexico.

Precious stones formed an important part of the tribute list: gold, turquoise, and jades are listed; gourds, copal for incense, copper, shells, skins and bird feathers, dye-stuffs, cotton, rubber—all were part of the economy. Chocolate, which every well-placed chieftain quaffed, flavored with honey, vanilla and, of all things, red pepper, must have come to Tenochtitlán in great quantities. "Moctezuma," wrote Bernal Díaz, "and his guests quaffed over 2,000 jugs . . . all frothed up." Foodstuffs were a dominant item in the tribute rolls; one can see very clearly the quantities of corn, beans, pepper, honey, vanilla, that made their way into the Aztec capital.

The *calpixque*, tribute-collectors, were naturally hated and feared. Their arrival every six months to supervise collections meant that towns had to disgorge much of their surplus. A good description of the *calpixque* is in the literature; they appeared in 1519 at the selfsame Totonac villages in Vera Cruz then occupied by Hernán Cortés and his small army: "Five Mexicans, who were Moctezuma's tax gatherers, had arrived. . . . They approached with utmost assurance and arrogance. . . . Their cloaks and loin-cloths were rich embroidered and their shining hair was gathered up as though tied on their heads and each was smelling a nosegay of flowers and each had a crooked staff in his hand. . . . Their Indian servants carried fly-whisks. . . ."

The Vera Cruz area was garrisoned by Aztec warriors; some were at Ceycoccnacan, said Hernán Cortés, "a fortified town which belongs to Moctezuma," so that any discourtesy to the tribute-collectors or any delay could bring swift retribution.

To give historical balance, not all tribes nor all towns under Aztec dominance were in opposition; the Aztec overlords freed them from the petty tribal struggles, commerce widened, prosperity was heightened by protection, roads were freed from attack and Tenochtitlán was a good consumer. Many accepted the Aztec peace willingly.

Who had title to the tribute and how did it enter their economy? Presumably the state, i.e., the First Speaker, who officially received the tribute at his capital. There, as we know, it was entered into his "account books." Some of it, such as excess foodstuffs, must have been distributed to the various clans on arrival; some of it was stored in the official storage chambers to be used against periodic famine or to pay, in lieu of money, the wages of those specialists attached to the royal household. Bernal Díaz said that "Moctezuma has two houses full of every sort of arms and shields and broad swords . . . that cut like razors . . . quilted cotton armour . . . casques or helmets of wood or bone . . . all the things that appeared on the tribute-lists."

Distribution of all this was made on a per capita basis. Aztec society existed for the good of the whole people, and while the tribute won by Aztec armies was in practice held by the "First Speaker," all of it, in one way or another, found its way back to the people. Arms were distributed to each clan and held in part of the local temple; foodstuffs were distributed. Doubtlessly, based on the designs of the shields, each clan had the right to ask a tributary village to make shields carrying their own coat of arms on it. Some of the tribute was used to pay the tax-free artisans, the specialists— priests, masons, goldsmiths, feather-workers, sculptors, etc. —who produced the vast array of beauty which the public enjoyed.

Such a tribute-state is not new in history; as has been pointed out, it has its parallel in Sumer, which, around 3000 B.C., maintained itself similarly. Before 2500 B.C. all the temple-cities of Mesopotamia within the same general region had been independent states until Sargon of Agade extended his conquests "to the silver mountain and the cedar forest," making, like the Aztec, a conquest of all the petty states and forcing tribute from them in the form of raw materials, and this imperialism "became a new instrument in the concentration of a still vaster social surplus." [112]

It was not enough that the Aztec was a tribute-state, for while the common man did not own land, he owned—after work-tax—the usufruct of the worked lands. Surplus was traded at the various markets, leisure time used up the raw materials which filtered down from top to bottom and were made into manufactured goods for "export" trade. So, to extend this economy, a new class came into being—something unknown among nations of other indigenous "American" organizations—a merchant class.

33. *Pochtecatl:* The Merchant Princes

The guilds of "commercial travelers," the *pochteca*, were a law unto themselves. They had distinct prerogatives. They lived in their own wards or *calpulli* (Pochtlan was one); guild rights passed from father to son; they paid no taxes; they had their own gods, and before setting off on a long journey they evoked the protection of Zacazontli, the protector of roads and travelers; and they were not subject to the ordinary law tribunals.

The *pochteca* were a rather late development in Aztec society; their history says "commerce began in Mexico-Tenochtitlán in the year 1504"; assuredly it was earlier. It rose out of the great social surplus piled up in the city as a

Fig. 50. The *pochteca* were commercial travelers of the imperial Aztec. With the aid of their human carriers, they extended Aztec commerce as far south as Nicaragua.

result first of tribute and then of the manufacturing activities of a people somewhat relieved from constant attention to agriculture. In and about the city the manufactured cotton cloth, rabbit-fur robes, obsidian and copper mirrors, cosmetics (a tincture of cochineal with grease) for face painting, medicinal herbs, flower pastes as a base for perfumes. Salt, which they leached out of the lakes, and other stuff that was light for long travel, were also in the list. For these things the directing classes and the common man alike wanted in return, from the hotlands, cotton, feathers, precious stones, chocolate, rubber. The *pochteca* were purveyors of luxuries.

All of the early Old World routes were luxury routes: the Amber road (still known as the *Birnsteinstrasse* where it passes through Bamberg, Germany) was the longest haul in ancient times—from Egypt to the Baltic. From 10,000 B.C. people journeyed these thousands of miles to obtain "Amber, that special act of God."

Salt, for many a luxury, made one of the great life-lines in history. The *Via Salaria* from Rome to Ostia was one of the first Roman roads. Grain eaters needed salt, for them it was an essential. Those in highland Mexico who had no coastal connections were dependent on the Aztec who controlled the salt-leaching works about the saline lakes. One of the plaints of the chieftains of the Tlascalans, hereditary enemies of the Aztec, was that "they had no salt; since there was none on their lands and they did not venture out."

Still the greatest traffic has always lain in luxuries. It was frankincense and myrrh, or silk loaded on camel caravans, or delicacies for "frolicking and chewing and sucking" for Greek or Roman banquets. In the New World the Aztec craved chocolate and feathers, jade, emeralds and gold dust. The man who said, "Give us luxuries and we will make them into necessities," points up Aztec appetites; the *pochteca* in this world were the alchemists turning the base metal of necessities into the gold of luxuries.

Trade was a monopoly of the *pochteca*. Days, weeks, months, were spent by them acquiring the articles for trade at the various markets; they then assembled carriers who were capable of carrying 60 pounds on their backs and the human caravan set off. In regions where conditions were not fully secure they were accompanied by Aztec warriors. Trade has always been sacrosanct. The way to bring down swift reprisal was to plunder them. If one of their numbers died in a far-off land he was given the same rites as a warrior slain in battle.

Aztec trading colonies under the *pochteca* penetrated to

Guatemala, going down the Pacific coast (which was not controlled by the Maya) as far south as Nicaragua. Their caravans were often gone for the fullness of two years. They also left colonists behind, small "islands" of Nahuatl-speaking peoples called *pipil*, who, even now, show their Nahuatl origin by their designs on pottery and weaving and the symbol of Tlaloc, the Aztec rain-god.[113]

The *pochteca* were often accused of being "warriors in disguise," ferreting out information as to the weakness and strength of tribes outside the pale of Aztec dominance. There seems to be no direct evidence of this, but as conquest often followed their trading incursions, the "other peoples" received them suspiciously when they bore gifts.

34. Roads, Transport, Couriers

Little is known of Aztec roads or communications. That there *were* roads and good communications must be assumed. Yet there have been no connected studies of Aztec roads such as have been made of the network of the Maya *sacbeoob,* nor has there been such an extensive survey as the von Hagen expedition study of the Inca highways on the west coast of Peru.[114]

The best-known Aztec road, since it was the one that Cortés and his small army followed from the hotlands to the uplands of Mexico, was that which ran from Vera Cruz to Mexico-Tenochtitlán; the precise route has been identified. The first prerequisite of empire is communications. Rome had it, the Inca had it, but since the Aztec was not an empire their roads were undeveloped. The nature of Mexican geography worked, it is true, against direct communications, and the engineering science of the Aztec was not oriented in the manner of Peru. Yet the Inca would have found Mexico's obstacles minor; they had roads that crossed the bare Andes as high as 15,000 feet.

Roads in Mexico followed the path of least resistance. The ancient trade route was on the warm Gulf Coast, the main road which ran from Xicalango (Sahagun called it "the land of Anáhuac Xicalango") as far north as the Tropic of Capricorn. Xicalango was located in the Laguna de Terminos, into which four rivers debouch. Here Maya trading missions had contact with central Mexican tribes. It is from here that Toltec troops were introduced into Yucatan in the twelfth century; it was from Xicalango that the Aztec had first news of the arrival of white man.* It was one of the great trading centers of Central Mexico; trade from Yucatan and Central America was brought to it by giant canoes arriving along the coast.

* "They had news of the arrival of the Christians from some merchants [*pochteca*] who had gone to the markets of these coasts . . . at Xilanco [Xicalango]. . . ."

The road ran northwest from here along the jungle coast through the Olmec country into the lands of the Totonac where a road (followed by Hernán Cortés and his small army) led to their villages, and to the large city of Cempoala. It is undescribed. There were no bridges—rivers which rose with callous ease would not permit them—natives crossed by canoes or by swimming. In fact in all Mexican literature there are no descriptions of bridges other than the small removable ones used by the Aztec in their causeways. Presumably this coastal road continued up as far as Tampico (22 degrees north latitude).

Mexico-Tenochtitlán was connected with a road from Vera Cruz and the conquistadors followed it. Only from them do we have a description: "The way was rugged"—understandably, since it rose from sea level to 8,000 feet; in a few miles it was narrow. In the heights when they entered Xicochimalco it was defended by "a town of great strength" and the road "was a narrow defile cut in steps." Beyond this the road passed through the frigid unpopulated heights of Cerro de Porote (13,000 feet) where the traveler was assailed by "whirlwinds of hailstones and rain."

Once the land mass lowered into a warmer plateau Cortés speaks of a "royal road"—it is not further described. They

Fig. 51. Courier-runners employed to carry messages over Aztec roads.

found rest-houses at intervals and occasionally small temples "with idols" which Cortés likened to roadside chapels built along Spanish roads. Near to Cholula they found two roads: "The best road was by way of Cholula," now the city of Puebla. This "royal road" passed between the volcanoes of Popocatepetl and Ixtaccihuatl ("my men proceeded along it until they came to two mountains between which it runs"), and went straight to Mexico-Tenochtitlán by way of the town of Amecameca; another branched off to Chalco near to the lake's edge and it was "well swept and clear."

Along this route, which is often subject to sleet and snow in the winter, there were houses like the Inca *tampus:* "groups of houses which they build like inns or hostels where the Indian traders lodge." At the edge of the lake they entered the wide causeways which lead to the capital of the Aztec.

Some of the Aztec roads were doubtlessly paved with *tzontli,* a pink pumice traprock, abundant and easily worked, composed of silica and volcanic ash. This is suggested by the fact that the name of the god of the road whom all travelers invoked was Zacazontli. But there is little physical evidence of pre-Hispanic paved roads throughout Mexico. There are remains of ceremonial ways at Teotihuacan; there is a sixty-foot broad paved road at Xochicalco that leads to a hilltop temple, but it is only half a mile in length. There is nothing like the Maya *sacbeoob,* "artificial road," built of limestone with a width of 15 feet, rising above the plain and extending for 62.3 miles from Coba to Yaxuna in Yucatan.[115]

Two roads went southwest out of Mexico-Tenochtitlán. One was that already described which ran through the snow-topped volcanoes to Cholula and on southward to Oaxaca toward the Pacific; the other leaving Mexico went due west of Cuernavaca and paralleled the first to Oaxaca, making junction at Huajolotitlán; it then proceeded to the Pacific Ocean, terminating at Huatulco. There seems not to have been any direct Aztec communication to the Pacific coast; indeed, there was no need. The Aztec did not use the sea; they had no maritime connection with any other land and there is no evidence of any direct communication, to use an example, between Mexico and Peru. All the evidence has been sifted; there were no communications between the Inca empire (or those that preceded it) and the cultures of Mexico. The Spaniard had to develop Mexico-Peru communications *ab ovo.*

The southern communications of the Aztec—a mere development from existing older routes—we know only because Hernán Cortés after his Mexican conquest used the road, enlarged it, and created a port at the Indian fishing village of Huatulco on the Pacific (the best natural port southward from Acapulco). The manner in which Cortés enlarged the ancient trails to provide space for cart-traffic suggests how it was done under the Aztec. The work of building and maintaining the roads, writes Dr. Woodrow Borah,[116] who was the first to thread his way through the maze to plot the road, was carried out by corvée levied on Indian towns near by. Each village took care of the twenty-mile section nearest it. They also maintained the inns or *mesones* on the route. The southbound Aztec-Zapotec road joined up with another transcontinental route at Tehuantepec, which crossed the flat isthmus at sea level. Where precisely the southbound road went from there is conjectural; our map must be regarded as schematic.

The Aztec was his own draft animal. Nothing new in this as man always was the first carrier. He made the first real roads, he could tire out the strongest animal, he could bear extremes of cold, hunger and thirst. Although the Aztec reached considerable heights in luxury, he never escaped carrying his own burdens. The llama and its relatives were unknown in Mexico until the estate of Hernán Cortés (Mar-

Fig. 52. Water transport was limited to lakes. The canoes were as large as the trees which could be brought down. Although the Aztec had some coastal trade, this was usually carried on by allied tribes.

quisate del Valle) brought a herd of sixty llamas *"ovejas del Perú."* They were taken to the highlands of Penol del Xico for domestication in Mexico; they died out and that was all. Although most carried their own produce, there were Indians of the baser sort who formed the human caravans. These *tamenes* were well-known; Bernal Díaz called them *"hombres de carga."* "There arrived 30 cargo-Indians called *tamenes.* . . ." The regular accepted weight was a little less than 60 pounds, the rate of travel 15 miles a day.

The wheel, except as used in children's toys, was totally absent in Mexico. The whole principle of the wheel as arch was unknown, as was the potter's wheel and the rotary quern. Even if the wheel had been known, it is doubtful that it could have served much without dray-animals. Instead the Aztec used the litter. This conveyance for the exalted was universal in the Old World as well as the New; few advanced cultures were without it. The Aztec seem to have considered it only a ceremonial device and not, as among the Inca and the Chimu in South America, a mode of transport. Moctezuma first appeared to the Spanish being carried in a litter along the great causeways out of the city; there is no mention, however, of the litter's being used beyond this; when Cortés took the unfortunate last Aztec "king" Cahuatemoc along on his expedition to Honduras, he walked as did the rest of the Indians.

Water transport was limited to the lakes. The Aztec constructed dugout canoes—almost everyone seems to have had one in this Venice-like city; much of the lacustrine commerce was carried on by water. Canoes brought in produce. They removed the excreta from the public toilets so as not to pollute the city and to use it for fertilizer. There were special canoes used to transport fresh water: "The water is sold from canoes," wrote Hernán Cortés. "The canoes place themselves under the bridges where the aqueducts are to be found . . . filled by men who are specially paid for this work." The Aztec used no other type larger than the dugout; when Cortés built two moderate-sized sloops on the lakes of Mexico he took the captive Moctezuma for a sail to a distant isle, skimming over the wind-swept waters, so that "Moctezuma was charmed and said that it was a great thing, this combining sails and oars together." The Aztec had nothing larger than these for the Pacific; in the Gulf the Maya had enormous dugouts and Caribs sailed the turbulent seas with no difficulty, but the Aztec, like the Inca, was a landlubber.

Couriers were employed on the roads to carry messages. Beyond the fact that they existed there is little more reference to them, whereas those Spaniards who went from Mexico to

Peru were astounded at the Inca system of *chasquis*, who, running in relays, could cover a distance of 1,250 miles in five days. The Aztec courier was trained to run; there were competitions for the fleet of foot and this tradition is still kept up by the present-day Tarahumara Indians living in Chihuahua.

Pictographic communications were put into a forked stick. It is not known for certain but it is probable that an artist accompanied the runners on important missions. Cortés was amazed at Vera Cruz upon receiving an embassy from Moctezuma that they "brought with them some clever painters, ordered them to make pictures true to nature of the face and body of Cortés and of the soldiers, ships, sails and horses, even of the two greyhounds and the cannon and cannon-balls." Later he found when in Mexico that Moctezuma had known by such means every action of theirs since they touched the shores of Mexico.

Thus the Aztec had roads, wayside rest-houses, roadside gods, couriers, and, through their pictographic writing, a good form of communications. The Europe of 1519 had not as much. "To journey in Europe," wrote Awaliyal Effendi in 1611, ". . . is like a fragment of hell." Roads in the sixteenth century were paved like hell in the proverb, and many the complaint that travel was a purgatory "in little." To move over Europe's roads one had to have "a falcon's eye, an ass's ears, a monkey's face, a merchant's words, a camel's back, a hog's mouth, a deer's feet."

It is small wonder that the conquistadors praised the Aztec roads.

35. Paper, Writing, Literature

All advanced civilizations (with the amazing exception of South American cultures such as the Inca, Chimu, Mochica and Tiahuanacu) had some form of paper, some form of writing, and some form of literature. In all these phases of culture the Aztec excelled.

Paper (*amatl*) was an article of tribute.

On the tribute-lists of Moctezuma one reads: "24,000 reams of paper are to be brought as a tribute yearly to Tenochtitlán." Twenty-four thousand reams would be 480,000 sheets of paper and judged by any standard this is an enormous consumption of paper.*

While it is not necessarily true, as someone once wrote, that the quantity of paper consumed stands in direct ratio to the intellectual development of a people, still the prevalence of paper and writing had much to do with the particular intellectual direction of the Aztec.

"True paper" (the product of a technique by which beaten fibrous material is felted on a mold while suspended in water) was not the paper of the Aztec. The inventors of true paper were the Chinese in A.D. 105. They used the fibers of the mulberry. The technique was transmitted by Chinese papermakers captured by the Arabs in 751 after the battle of Samarkand. Papermaking was perfected by the Arabs, brought by them to Spain in 1150 when they settled in Xativa, from whence paper went around the Western world.[117] The Egyptians did not have "true paper" either; papyrus was made by laminating strips of the stems of a water plant; they were able to produce rolls of papyrus "paper" 12 inches wide, 40 feet long. The most widely used method of obtaining a paper substitute, the one used by peoples in such widely separated regions as Polynesia, Melanesia, Southern Asia, Africa, South America, and the

---

* "Ream" is adapted from the Spanish *resma*, which in turn is derived from the arabic *rizmah*, "a bundle, especially of paper." It is only an expression which fortuitously coincided with the Aztec numeral *pilli*.

method that was the source of Maya and Aztec paper, was the technique of peeling off the bark of the *ficus,* related to the mulberry, and felting it into sheets as thin as paper by beating it with a ribbed mallet. This is called "bark cloth," but it is not cloth since it is not woven; it is bark-paper.

A functional form of paper made in this manner appeared very early in Yucatan and Mexico. There is no manner of dating its appearance but von Hagen, who did the pioneer work on it, is of the opinion that it was used as paper among the Maya as early as 1000 B.C.[118] The Maya folded their *huun*-paper and made polychromic books of it. The paper prepared from the inner bast fibers of the wild fig trees was, in use and appearance, like true paper. There are only three such Maya "books" or codices left of those that escaped the "burning of the books" in Yucatan by Bishop Diego de Landa.

All of the advanced cultures in Mexico had paper and writing. The Toltec had glyph writing and the same graphic techniques; they are credited with having in the seventh century an encyclopedic *teoamextli,* a divine book compiled in A.D. 660; neither it nor others like it have survived. The Mixtec at Cholula had paper and writing; several of their book-codices are extant. So did the Zapotec in Oaxaca and the Totonac in Vera Cruz. Bernal Díaz saw piles of books near the Totonac city-state of Cempoala: "When we came on many towns . . . and found idol houses . . . and many paper books doubled together in folds like cloth of Castile."

Paper and writing, then, were not an Aztec invention; the Aztec, however, perfected them.

The fact that the Indians had books and writing greatly astonished the conquistador: "There is so much to think over," said Bernal Díaz, "that I do not know how to describe it, seeing things as we did that had never been heard or seen before or even dreamed about." So much so that they sent back to Spain along with the first gold collected two of such books. Fortunately these fell into the hands of the Italian humanist Pietro Martire d'Anghiera, who was then in Seville; he, corresponding with the learned, wrote about "books such as the Indians use." Later Dr. Francisco Hernández, in 1570, who was neither priest nor clerk, came to Mexico in the capacity of *proto-médico* on the first botanical expedition to the new world.[119] In the course of his five-year plant explorations he saw the paper-craft at Tetoztlan: "Many Indians are employed at this craft. . . . The sheets of paper are then polished (by means of a *xicaltetl*) and fashioned into sheets." These *xicaltetl* were stone flat-iron shaped celts which, when heated and pressed upon the paper, closed the pores and gave it surface;

more or less the same technique that European papermakers during the Renaissance used to burnish paper by means of an agate stone. "It is something like our own paper," he wrote, "except that theirs is whiter and thicker." The paper was called *amatl,* the tree the *amaqua-huitl* (literally: "paper-tree"), of the genus *Ficus.*

The Aztec glyph for *amatl* was a roll. Yet there were other types. A yellow paper always sold in sheets came from the town of Amacoztitlan on the Rio Amacuzac in the State of Morelos; it derives from the fibers of the yellow wild fig, the *Ficus petiolaris.* This whole area, in a tropical setting of under 5,000 feet, was *the* paper manufacturing center of ancient Mexico. Itzamatitlan, a village in Morelos on the Rio Yuatepec, was the source of yet another type of paper.

Aside from its intellectual use, this immense consumption of paper passed into the lives of the people. The Aztec were as the Chinese in this respect in their reverence for paper, for "All classes of Chinese," writes Dard Hunter,[120] "from the aristocratic scholar . . . down to the most illiterate coolie, a

Fig. 53. Two forms of Aztec papermaking. On the left, an Indian pulls off the bark of the wild Ficus tree (related to the mulberry which is also used in papermaking). The bark was then beaten into large rolls of paper which were folded double to make books. On the right, a woman makes smaller pieces of paper from branch fibers of the same tree.

pronounced reverence for every scrap of paper." This, more or less, was the attitude of the Aztec.

Paper on arrival went first to the priests, writers, artists, then it passed into the market where it was purchased or traded. Bernal Díaz saw it there: "There was paper, which in this country is called *amatl*." Sahagun, the observant Franciscan monk, in his great work on the Aztec in the chapter entitled "The Gods Which the Ancient Mexicans Adored" tells us that "for the merchant's god Yacatecuhtli . . . they made offerings of paper . . . for the image of *Napatecli*—the patron god of the rush-mat makers—they gave him a crown of paper . . . and in his hands flowers made of paper." Each of the Aztec months dedicated to a god was "honoured by strips of paper covered with copal and rubber . . . for the goddess who lived in the house of the sun . . . they adorned with paper." So it went on, every phase of life or worship used *amatl*-paper. Even today the descendants of the Otomis remain papermakers. They make their paper from the same plants as did the Aztec.

The greater bulk of the paper, however, was used to keep the genealogies, trial records, land records, for each ward or *calpulli* had its land registers and tribute rolls. There were hundreds, perhaps thousands, of such "books." Bernal Díaz thumbed through them when he wandered into the endless rooms of Moctezuma's palace; he followed an "accountant" and he saw "all the revenue that was brought . . . and recorded in his books which were made of a paper which they call amatl . . . and he had a great house full of these books."

Those not destroyed by the Spanish siege of Mexico perished in other ways. After the Conquest Fray Juan de Zumarraga collected all the "books" that could be found, especially the "royal library" at Texcoco, east of Mexico, and "the most cultivated capital of Anáhuac," wrote Prescott, "and the great repository of the national archives." Monks began the "burning of the books"; only a pitiful fourteen now remain.

Aztec writing was non-phonetic, like all early writing. It was not capable of any general statement nor could concrete ideas be expressed. Only in its later evolution was a change sensed and the Aztec seemed to be arriving at the beginning of syllabic phonetics. This would have occurred when signs no longer stood for pictures or even ideas, but sounds. Instead, Aztec writing, in 1519, was still pictographic: a wrapped mummy figure was a symbol of death; migrations or movements along the road were expressed by footprints; seeing was expressed by an eye projected beyond the viewer; speaking was a wagging tongue; a mountain was symbolized

1

2

Fig. 54. Three types of Aztec *amatl*-paper. (1) A paper roll attached to the symbol for 8,000. (2) A yellow paper, made in sheets, which came from the town of Amacoztitlan. Above the paper is the teeth-symbol for *tlan*-place; below, the symbol for water. (3) A long roll-paper, which came from the town of Itzamatitlán, made from the Ficus tree, whose leaf was shaped like a dagger *(itzli)*.

3

so obviously that even one untrained in reading Aztec glyphs would know it. These symbols could be compounded so that if a "rememberer" wished to chant of a notable historical fact such as *"In the year 2-Reed (1507) Moctezuma conquered the village of Itztepec,"* the *tlacuilo*-artist would have first drawn the year 2-Reed, then the official accepted symbol of Moctezuma, a thin line would have run to a burning temple and above it the rebus drawing of the town of Itztepec (an obsidian dagger on top of a mountain).

There was naturally no alphabet to this system, yet the Aztec did combine a series of pictorial elements, often in abstract, to give complicated meanings; by these methods as well as by puns, color, position, they produced a staggering amount of records.

God and the exigencies of economy were the motifs for the development of writing; at least this was true in the Near East. Early Sumerian writing (about 5000 B.C.) developed as did the Aztec. The clay tablets were impressed, says Dr. H. S. Hooke in the *History of Technology*,[121] with a cow's head, an ear of grain, a fish, a mound; later they were compounded and show the "first attempts to express verbal notions." By 4000 B.C. the Sumerians had a syllabary or sign-list of 500-600 signs. Egyptian writing developed similarly. The motive that furthered writing was the need to record tribute. In the temple-cities of the Near East, God was regarded as the owner of the land and the people as occupiers of the land and they had to pay rent to the temple-city, to the priests who were the gods' vicars.

In the beginning early Egyptian pictorial writing differed not overly from that of the Aztec. Later, in the Middle Kingdom, it was reduced to 732 conventional signs, moved into syllabary, developed homonyms, and, as it progressed, divorced sound from meaning. Still later it evolved into a cursive form of glyphic script and by 800 B.C. into demotic, which is the form found on the Rosetta Stone. In the beginning the pictographic glyph to express a historical event was not much different. Take for example an historical event of King Narmer's dated 3100 B.C.[122] This is a mixture of pictorial and phonetic elements: *"Horus brings to the Pharaoh 6,000 foreigners captured within their land."* When placed alongside the historical event contrived to show the working of Aztec writing, it exhibits the same quality of writing evolution.

This speaks very well for the perception of the Aztec, for although his cultural attainments appeared 4,500 years later in time than the Egyptian, it must be remembered that man migrated to the "Americas" during the early Neolithic

Fig. 55. An illustration showing the comparative glyph-writing of Egyptian and Aztec. Above: A detail from King Narmer's palette, Hierakonpolis, Egypt, 3100 B.C. The first sign of the man symbolizes a fish, the n'r fish and its phonetic value *Nar*. The second sign represents a chisel, *mer;* hence the name of the king, Narmer. Narmer holds a warrior by the hair—the symbol of captivity. Above this a falcon sits on six lotus buds. Each lotus (kha) has the sound value of 1,000. So it is read: "King Narmer brings 6,000 foreigners captured with their hand." Below: An arrangement of Aztec history, as given in the *Codice Mendocino,* to show similar thought and glyphic pattern. This depicts one of the military achievements of Moctezuma I (surnamed "The Wrathy"), 1440-69. A rebus drawing of his name is above. An Aztec grabs the hair of another—the symbol of battle. To the right is a symbol of a temple on fire, meaning conquest; attached to the temple is the rebus drawing of the village, a tree which has a speaking tongue—Quanahuaca (modern Cuernavaca). Above it is the date, 2-Acatl, 1469.

stage of man's history. At the time of his arrival the other Neolithic cultures, Mid-East, Europe, Greece, had no greater wit nor ornament. But the "American" became isolated from the main currents of cultural evolution. Writing, the wheel, the alphabet, metalworking, etc., came out of the "fertile crescent" and from it made its way throughout the Old World. Even then diffusion worked slowly. It took 2,000 years for the wheel to reach Britain and other inventions were even longer in arriving.

"The fabric of the Old World history," writes Pál Kelemen, "is like a vast web stretching from the Roman ramparts of England to the delicately drawn woodcuts of Japan, from the Byzantine icons of the Russian steppes to the wondrous world of the royal tombs of Egypt. . . . It is an enormous territory . . . yet remote as certain points lie from one another, as different the styles, it is clear that details and even whole ideas were incorporated, adapted and developed inter-regionally.[123]

The Aztec had literature. The term perhaps is incorrect, just as saying that their functional crafts were "art" is not wholly right; while both expressions are true, they are in fact misleading. As is obvious, the Aztec had no literature as we understand it, even though the word can be defined as "the total of preserved writings belonging to a given language or people." Yet, since one must always put a truth or a conclusion at the end of a chain of reasoning, like the knot at the end of a thread—since otherwise the knot would not hold—so then Aztec literature. . . .

It was mostly history. Annals of ancient times, year-counts, books of the day and the hours—even diaries. There were observations of planetary events, eclipses, movements of stars, observations of celestial phenomena which had affected or might affect their present. There was much out of the past; their mythopoetic faculty was well developed. They were poets and most delighted when writing and singing of the past— for only the past is really poetic. One of their chief concerns was this; their "histories," recorded on paper, showed the migrations, the stopping-off places, the wars, conflicts, founding of cities. Their sacred almanacs were scarcely literature nor were their tribal records, land registers, lines of descent and tribute charts.

Their history approached more closely to what we know as literature. Even then, what was put down was only enough to aid the memory; there were no cross-references to other tribes. The Aztec seem to any who read their glyphic charts as if they lived alone in Mexico. No reference is made to other tribes. Aztec interests extended "vertically from tribe to pantheon."

Aztec literature really consisted of that which was unwritten, that which was transmitted orally, and this glyph writing served to provoke the memory of the "rememberers." This helped them to recall the passing of events and these twice-told sagas, hymns, elegies, chants, only became "literature" when they were set down by a bilingual scribe (Spanish-Nahuatl) after the Conquest.[124]

Many of the great sagas which form our world literature were mouth-transmitted before they were set down. For how long were the wanderings of Ulysses chanted before some nimble-fingered scrivener put it down? All the stories of the Cicones, the Lotophagi, the Cyclops, and the Laestrygones whom enchantresses took to their couch and who evoked the dead, were all repeated in chant before being made "immortal" by letters. The same with the Druids. The priests and medicine men of Celtic Britain were court bards whose function became to "celebrate the king's temporal power" in song and chant. Richard Coeur de Lion and Henry III employed a *versificator regis* who chanted rhymed chronicles in order to remember better "epitaphs and suchlike." The Welsh bards,[125] when they found vellum prohibitively dear, recorded their chronologies, their treaties on geography and husbandry, in mnemonic rhyme; their tales to be remembered totaled over 900.

And so with Aztec "literature." Present-day Mexican scholars who speak Nahuatl as easily as they do mellifluous Spanish have translated the original texts set down by scribes who transcribed them from the original sixteenth-century Nahuatl speech. Dr. Angel María Garibay has filled two volumes of things "Aztec" [126] (which are here translated into English for the first time) and it is amazing how wide the field of the Aztec concern was. Reading them we are brought in closer connection with these people whose spectacular history has here been set down. They were always curious about their relation to the universe as a whole, they questioned themselves about life and afterlife.

> Is it true that one lives only on earth?
> Not for ever on earth: only a short while here.
> Even jade will crack
> Even gold will break
> Even quetzal feathers will rend,
> Not for ever on earth: only a short while here.

Those who may go into the place of the underworld chant about the day:

[If] in one day we leave
In one night descend to the mysterious regions,
Here we only came to meet,
We are only passers-by on earth.
Let us pass life in peace and pleasure; come, let us rejoice.
But not those who live in wrath: the earth is very wide!
That one could live forever, that one need not die.

The poetic side of their lives, their imagery and the love of nature and flowers, which even Hernán Cortés first recognized, is expressed in an agony of soul:

My heart wishes with longing for flowers,
I suffer with the song, and only rehearse songs on earth,
I Cuacuauhtzin:
I want flowers that will endure in my hands . . . !
Where shall I gather beautiful flowers, beautiful songs?
Never does spring produce them here:
I alone torment myself, I Cuacuauhtzin.
Can you rejoice perchance, may our friends have pleasure?
Where shall I gather beautiful flowers, beautiful songs?

The Codice Florentino, written in Spanish, translated directly from ideographic Nahuatl speech, sermoned how the boys studying in the *calmecac* religious schools "must learn artfully all the songs, the songs of the gods . . . which are written in the books," such as these:

Where shall I go?
Where shall I go?
The road of the gods of duality,
Could your house perchance be the place of the fleshless?
Perchance inside heaven?
Or is only earth here,
The place of the fleshless?

and others which reaffirmed God's possession of this celestial globe:

In heaven you live;
The mountains you uphold,

> Anáhuac is in your hand,
> Everywhere, always you are awaited,
> You are invoked, you are entreated,
> Your glory, your fame are sought.
> In heaven you live:
> Anáhuac is in your hand.

One American scholar, John Cornyn, who has given a whole book to it in his Aztec literature, opines that in the whole range of indigenous "American" literature no other tribe has left such a variety of expressions and feelings. For it is through chants that literature left the realm of the priestly intellectual and entered the people. Here they stress ideas, both hieratic and secular, a fact unusual in itself. A poet, perhaps a worker in fine stones, sings of the beauty of gems:

> Jades I perforate, gold I cast in the crucible:
> This is my song!
> I set emeralds . . .
> This is my song.

and that he *felt* as a literate artist feels is expressed in this that when one creates, there is "God in his heart."

> The good painter;
> Toltec-artist of the black and red ink,
> Creator of things with the black water. . . .

> The good painter; understanding
> God in his heart,
> Defies things with his heart,
> Dialogues with his own heart.

> He knows colours, applies and shadows them.
> Draws the feet, the faces,
> Sketches the shadows, obtains a finish,
> As if he were a Toltec-artist
> He paints the total colours of flowers.

Does one suspect these sentiments? Does it appear that the original Nahuatl-Mexican text has been improved in the translation, gilded by Spanish poets who love to tint the past with new colors? This is how a fragment of the original text appears in parallel translation in the manuscript *Leyenda de los Soles* (Legend of the Suns)[127] which was set down originally in 1558:

	Ah tlamiz noxochiuh ah tla-
My flowers shall not perish	miz nocuic
Nor shall my chants cease	In noconehua
They spread, they scatter.	Xexelihui ya moyahua

Mexico, like Peru, was a sun-state. Above all was the sun-god and no matter how many the manifestations of the gods, how widespread their influence, the sum of all things came from the sun. Mexico was virtually a Sun Kingdom.

> Now our father the Sun
> Sinks attired in rich plumes,
> Within an urn of precious stones,
> As if girdled with turquoise necklaces goes,
> Among ceaselessly falling flowers. . . .

Such is an idea, an idea, nothing more, of Aztec literature. It has recently been carefully scrutinized by Dr. Miguel León Portilla in a book *La Filosofía Nahuatl*[128] (not available in English), which casts a new light on the human qualities of the Aztec. There is more Aztec literature extant than one would at first surmise, even though much has been lost. But what *is* here tallies very well with what the first conquistadors said they saw of Aztec life and what has been confirmed by archaeology.

As the world spun into 1519 the Aztec could look back on a history which for sheer will to power has few peers. They came out of nothing and made themselves in a relatively short time heirs of thousands of years of culture even greater than their own, a culture which was adopted and assimilated by them. They gave the Mexican land its first direction toward some form of economic synthesis. They gave it a new concept of commerce, by extending trade beyond traditional borders. Their knowledge of geography and of plants was vast. They developed paper into a veritable industry. They had writing which tended more and more to evolve into the phonetic. They had literature. They were using wooden and clay stamps to impress designs and symbols on their *amatl*-paper. Thus the

Aztec had all the ingredients—paper, writing, literature and stamping—which ancient China had and which brought about the first steps toward that reproduction of ideas by printing which extended civilization.

It is, however, useless to speculate what might have been. In that year of 1519 a small fleet of vessels anchored at Vera Cruz: Hernán Cortés had arrived.

36. Hail and Farewell

✦

They fell.

It is a drama which, no matter how often told, never seems to lose the patina of its metaled romance. The Spanish who took active part in it felt the historicity of the moment: Hernán Cortés penned his famous *Five Letters* even while wading through a sea of Aztec blood. Three other Spaniards who participated left their impressions as well, including that wonderful Bernal Díaz del Castillo, one who even at the age of eighty-four could not forget its impact: ". . . it all comes before my eyes as though it had happened yesterday." The Conquest will be a source for literature for a long time and none perhaps will replace William Prescott's historical narrative. All the others that have followed—be it General Lew Wallace, D. H. Lawrence, or Samuel Shellabarger, or even Madariaga's *Heart of Jade* and Maurice Collis's *Cortés and Moctezuma*—are only pallid copies of the original piece forged by William Prescott.

They fell. Why they fell can be found in the literature—it was inevitable. Once white man began to probe into the new world, contact with the Aztec and conquest of the Aztec were a certainty; if it had not been Hernán Cortés, it would have been someone else.

Hernán Cortés arrived at a psychological moment in Mexico (just as in Peru Francisco Pizarro came when the Incas had just gone through a civil war). A god, Quetzalcoatl, was expected from the east. Columbus made contact with the Maya in his fourth and last voyage in 1502. This amazing bit of intelligence, enlarged every time it was told and retold, came to the ears of Aztec merchants, who were trading near Yucatan at the ancient market of Xicalango at that time. Moctezuma came into power in 1503. During his reign white men continued to appear and disappear along the Gulf shores. Quetzalcoatl, the culture-hero of these "Americas," who was expelled from his land, vowed as he sailed away into that selfsame Gulf-sea that "on the date of my birth which is *Ce-Acatl*, the year of 1-Reed—*I will return*." According to the Aztec calendar this year 1-Reed could only fall, in the Christian calendar reckoning, in the years 1363, 1467, or 1519. In 1519 Hernán Cortés appeared on the shores of Vera Cruz and one of the first gifts sent to him by Moctezuma was a magnificent headdress of quetzal plumes, the same headdress which today is in the Museum at Vienna. Long before this the whole Aztec people had gone through years of tribulations; they felt their insecurity as their priests searched the heavens and the earth for portents of disaster. Long columns of sacrificial victims were taken from tribute villages and immolated on the sacrificial block so that the gods might bring them answers to their questionings about the strange creatures that were appearing and disappearing on their shores. It was natural that these demands upon other tribes for sacrificial victims would alienate them; even those tribes who had been friendly for two hundred years were desperately angry over the drain on their own kin; bonds between conqueror and conquered were loosened. But the Aztec in fear and uncertainty increased the pressure.

Then Hernán Cortés appeared. He came with new weapons, horses, steel armor, and new gods. Two different worlds, two different human natures, met. The Aztec had no concept of himself as a separate absolute entity, he thought in terms of clan; the Spaniard believed in his own person, the most real reality of his world was his own individual soul.[129]

They fell. They fell, suggests William Prescott, under the weight of a different, "if not in some respects higher, civilization; none of its achievements could save it and its own internal weaknesses helped to destroy it." Moral history is not good history; historical action, judged under the Spinozan "aspect of eternity," lies beyond good and evil. By its very nature history is amoral, and yet. . . .

And yet what Prescott wrote bears some relation to the reality of the facts of this book: "The Aztec monarchy fell by the hand of its own subjects. . . . Its fate may serve as a striking proof that a government which does not rest on the sympathies of its subjects cannot long abide; that human institutions, when not connected with human prosperity and progress, must fall . . . by the hand of violence from within or from without."

Thus on Saint Hippolytus' Day, August 13, 1521, in the stench of a thousand fires, the Spanish Conquest was complete and the Aztec passed into cultural limbo.

BIBLIOGRAPHY AND NOTES

1. Maurice Collis, *Cortés and Montezuma,* London: Faber & Faber, Ltd., 1954.
   The latest interpretation, by a well-known English writer, of the strange relationship between Montezuma and Hernán Cortés. Well-guided by Aztec specialists, the author has given a new twist to the old facts.

2. William H. Prescott, *History of the Conquest of Mexico,* New York: Harper & Brothers, 1843.
   This work has withstood a century of siege, from all quarters. It still remains, since Prescott worked from original sources and knew how to thread his way between fact and fiction, the best over-all history of the conquest of Mexico. New material has altered it, new evidence and discoveries have augmented it, but it remains the master work.

3. Hernando Cortés, *Five Letters, 1519–1526,* tr. by J. Bayard Morris, London: G. Routledge & Sons, 1928; New York: R. M. McBride & Co., 1929.
   The five letters were written between 1519 and 1526. In Spanish they were termed *Cartas-Relaciones,* half-letters, half-dispatches. These could not be called literary masterpieces, still many were penned in the heat of battle—and bear this imprint. Two of them were published in 1524 in Nuremberg with the only plan of the city of Tenochtitlán as it was in 1519.

4. Anonymous Conqueror, *Narrative of Some Things of New Spain and of the Great City of Temestitan,* tr. by Marshall Saville, New York: The Cortés Society, 1917.
   Not easily available, since it has been reprinted in only limited editions, this short work by one who was anonymous and communal should be read alongside that of Bernal Díaz del Castillo and the letters of Cortés, to gain a full-sided picture of the impact of the conquest on Aztec—and Spaniard.

5. Andres de Tapia, *Relación hecha por Andres de Tapia sobre la Conquista de México. Col. de Documentos para la Historia de México,* t. 11, Mexico, 1866.

6. Francisco López de Gómara, *Crónica de la Nueva España, con la Conquista de México . . . hechos por el valeroso Hernando Cortés, Marqués del Valle,* Zaragoza, 1552.

7. Bernal Díaz del Castillo, *The Discovery and Conquest of Mexico, 1517–1521,* tr. by A. P. Maudslay, New York: Farrar, Straus & Cudahy, 1956.
   Since it is an honest work and deals with people—the basic foundation of history—Bernal Díaz's is a rich tapestry of human events. Its vitality is attested by the continuously new editions that appear.

8. Bernardino de Sahagun, *A History of Ancient Mexico,* tr. by Fanny R. Bandelier, Nashville: Fisk University Press, 1932.
   Sahagun came early to Mexico (1595) while the Aztec traditions were still alive. The work is wonderfully detailed (there are accompanying illustrations which do not appear in all the publications) and it is an honest attempt at reportage. The English edition was prepared by Fanny Bandelier, the widow of Adolph Bandelier, one of the pioneers in American Indian studies.

9. Toribio de Benavente o Motolinía, *Historia de los Indios de la Nueva España,* Barcelona: Herederos de Juan Gili, 1914. Written in the sixteenth century.
   Juan de Torquemada, *Veintiún Libros Rituales y Monarquía Indiana,* Madrid, 1723.

10. Francisco Hernández, *Rerum Medicarum Novae Hispaniae Thesaurus seu Plantarum,* Rome, 1649.
    The work of the great Spanish proto-medico Francisco Hernández (see his brief biography by von Hagen) who came to Mexico during the years 1570–75; with his Aztec assistants, he filled 16 folio volumes with drawings and descriptions of 3000 plants in Spanish, Nahuatl and Latin. Reduced to 1000 species, it was a gigantic herbal on Dioscoridean lines. Unpublished in his lifetime, this badly edited *Thesaurus* of 951 pages was printed in Rome.
    Victor W. von Hagen, "Francisco Hernández, Naturalist," *Scientific Monthly,* New York, 1944.

11. Constantin Volney, *Les Ruines: Un Méditation sur les Révolutions des Empires,* Paris, 1791.
    There is an English edition of *The Ruins* which was prepared by Count Volney himself. Although rhapsodic and, as archaeology, inaccurate, it still had great influence in France, England and the United States. It provided at this early date (1791) much stimulus toward interest in man's past.

12. Paganini Ricardo Castañeda, *Las Ruinas de Palenque*, Guatemala, 1946.

13. José Antonio Alzate, *Descripcion de las antiguedades de Xochicalco*, Mexico, 1791.
Xochicalco was one of the first Mexican sites to enter the literature. Although Humboldt did not visit it, he gathered the description made by Sr. Alzate with a drawing (something less than accurate) by F. Aguera done in 1791. This he published in his famous *Atlas Pittoresque* (Paris, 1810).

14. Victor W. von Hagen, *South America Called Them; Explorations of the Great Naturalists (La Condamine, Humboldt, Darwin and Spruce)*, New York: Alfred A. Knopf, 1945.

15. Alexander von Humboldt, *Vues des Cordillères et Monuments des Peuples Indigènes de l'Amérique*, Paris, 1810.
Humboldt was the great figure of the opening of the nineteenth century. After explorations in South America, Cuba and Mexico, he compiled a vast amount of data extraordinary in both its range and its accuracy. This work is a landmark in American archaeology but now little used since the volume is in folio and is expensive. Yet it deserves to be reconsidered. His attitude toward archaeological remains as fragments of history laid the solid base of American scholarship.

16. J. F. de Waldeck, *Voyage Pittoresque et Archéologique*, Paris, 1838.
That which Humboldt put forward, Waldeck retarded. Humboldt compiled evidence as to the American origin of the Indian; Waldeck, a brilliant draftsman, falsified Maya figures and hieroglyphics and gave "substance" to the vague Jewish origin of the American Indian. His title of "Count" was bogus, his personal history in great part an invention. We know that he lived in Paris, managed a silver mine at Tlalpujahna, and painted backdrops for the stage in Mexico, traveled in Yucatan and visited Palenque. "I have a soupçon," said Prescott, "that Waldeck was a good deal of a charlatan and that his colouring does not bear the true weather tints of antiquity." He was right. The book is beautiful, facile, and contrived.
For critical appraisal of Waldeck:
Victor W. von Hagen, "Waldeck," *Natural History Magazine*, New York, 1946.
Howard F. Cline, "The Apochryphal Early Career of Waldeck," *Acta Americana*, Vol. 4, No. 4, Mexico, 1947.

17. John Lloyd Stephens, *Incidents of Travel in Central America, Chiapas, and Yucatan,* 2 vols., New York: Harper & Brothers, 1841.
    This work is to all intents and purposes the first recording of the discovery of the great extent of the Maya. With its accurate yet dramatic drawings by Frederick Catherwood, it laid down the broad base of American archaeology. A lawyer, a non-professional, Stephens, with very little historical material available, nonetheless was amazingly accurate in his forecast of Maya history. A reprint is available (Rutgers University, 2 vols. 1949).
    See also:
    Victor W. von Hagen, *Maya Explorer: John Lloyd Stephens and the Lost Cities of Central America and Yucatan,* Norman: University of Oklahoma Press, 1947.
    ————, *Frederick Catherwood, Architect,* New York: Oxford University Press, 1950.

18. Edward King, Viscount Kingsborough, *Antiquities of Mexico,* 9 vols., London, 1830–48.
    Lord Kingsborough would have been sunk in the stream of time except that he published, at the cost of both life and fortune, this folio collection of nine volumes. The set is now eagerly sought by collectors and scholars since Lord Kingsborough reproduced many of the heretofore unpublished Mixtec, Aztec and Maya codices. The text, which is a potpourri of every unconsidered theory, attempts to prove in short that the American Indian descended from one of the Lost Tribes of Israel. He belonged to the lunatic fringe of archaeological enthusiasts. He died, quite undeservedly, in debtors' prison, because of his failure to pay for the paper that was used in this publication. Kingsborough belongs to history, but his history scarcely belongs to him.

19. A. P. Maudslay, *A Glimpse at Guatemala,* London: John Murray, 1899.
    Zelia Nuttall (ed. and tr.), *Codex Magliabecci, The Book of Life of the Ancient Mexicans, Containing an Account of Their Rites and Superstitions,* Berkeley: University of California Press, 1903.
    T. A. Joyce, *Mexican Archaeology,* London: P. L. Warner; New York: G. P. Putnam's Sons, 1914.
    A very successful attempt to portray the whole of the field of Mexican archaeology. A rare book when obtainable, and expensive.

20. Paul Kirchhoff, "Mesoamerica," *Acta Americana,* Vol 1, Mexico, 1943.

21. Jacques Soustelle, *La Vida Cotidiana de los Aztecas,* Mexico, 1955; *La Vie quotidienne des Aztèques a la veille de la conquête espagnole,* Paris: Hachette, 1955.
    The use of the pre-conquest and later post-conquest repertorial drawings of the Aztec to tell their own story. Written by a Frenchman, very expert in his field, with a new presentation. The book is available in French and Spanish, not yet in English.

22. Manuel Gamio, *La Población del Valle de Teotihuacán,* 3 vols., Mexico, 1922.
    Alfonso Caso, *El Pueblo del Sol,* Mexico, 1947.
    José García Payón, "Malinalco," *Rev. Mex. de Estudios Antropológicos,* Mexico, 1946.
    Eduardo Noguera, *Cerámica de México,* Mexico, 1932.
    Ignacio Marquina, *Arquitectura Prehispánica,* Mexico, 1951.

23. Victor W. von Hagen, *Aztec and Maya Papermakers,* New York: J. J. Augustin, 1943.
    ————, *Jungle in the Clouds (Search and Capture of the Quetzal-bird),* New York: Duell, Sloan & Pearce, 1940.
    ————, *Maya Explorer, op. cit.*
    ————, *Frederick Catherwood, Architect, op. cit.*

24. Oswald Spengler, *The Decline of the West,* tr. by Charles F. Atkinson, New York: Alfred A. Knopf, 1932.
    Despite the appearance of *A Study of History* by Arnold Toynbee, with the final hope of life being churchly Christian (Episcopalian, we hope) Spengler remains very cogent. His analysis of cultures is excellent and despite the gloomy forecast of the "decline" it still can be read, perhaps not with overmuch pleasure, yet with much intellectual profit.

25. Bernal Díaz del Castillo, *op. cit.*

26. Hernando Cortés, *op. cit.*

27. Gregorio García, *Origen de los Indios,* Madrid, 1732.
    This (written 1607) is one of the many, albeit better-known, theological proofs offered as to why the American "Indians are Jewes." He identifies the Biblical Ophir with Peru; Joktan of Genesis becomes Yucatan.

28. Fray Diego Durán, *Historia de las Indias de Nueva España,* 2 vols.—Atlas, Mexico, 1867–1880. Written in the sixteenth century.

29. Harmon L'Estrange, *Americans no Jewes,* London, 1652.

30. John L. Sorensen, "Some Mesoamerican Traditions of Immigration," *El México Antiguo,* Tomo viii, pp. 425–39, Mexico, 1955.
This was written by a resident of Utah and a Mormon. There are two aspects of this church, one the respected community of hard-working, God-fearing, God-in-my-heart people, and the other, the history-twisters. They attempt, as this book exemplifies, using every device in archaeology, to "prove" that the American Indians were Jews. Joseph Smith had revealed the Golden Tablets of the Book of Mormon in 1831. Moroni was an angel that appeared, a descendant of the Lost Tribes of Israel, from whom the American Indian has his origin. This is their theme and they are stuck with it. Any theory which advances the cause of "peopling the Americas" by sea, rafts, balsas, they pursue to delirium. Every natural and explainable Indian motif is transmuted into symbols which will prove the theme of "The American Indians are Jewes."

31. Philip Drucker, "Radiocarbon Dates from La Venta, Tabasco," *Science,* July 12, 1957, Vol. 126, No. 3263, pp. 72–73, Washington, 1957.

32. Miguel Covarrubias, *Mexico South: The Isthmus of Tehuantepec,* New York: Alfred A. Knopf, 1946; London: Cassell, 1947.
The late Miguel Covarrubias was by far and large more than a clever illustrator, he was an imaginative archaeologist. He wandered much over the Mexican scene and pursued archaeology; his belief that the Olmec would emerge as one of the earliest of the Mexican tribes has been borne out by radiocarbon dating.

33. Miguel Covarrubias, *op. cit.*

34. Matthew W. Stirling, "La Venta" in *Initial Series from Tres Zapotes, Vera Cruz and Mexico* (Mexican Archaeology Series, Vol. 1, No. 1), Washington: National Geographic Society, 1940.

35. Miguel Covarrubias, *op. cit.*

36. Fernando de Alva Ixtililoxochitl, *Obras Históricas,* 2 vols., Mexico, 1891–92. Written in the seventeenth century.

37. Gordon Ekholm, *Excavations at Tampico and Panuco in the Huasteca, Mexico* (Anthropological Papers, Vol. 38), New York: American Museum of Natural History, 1944.

38. *Ibid.*

39. Miguel Covarrubias, *op. cit.*

40. Sigvald Linné, *Archaeological Researches at Teotihuacán, Mexico,* New York and London: Oxford University Press, 1934.

41. George C. Vaillant, *The Aztecs of Mexico,* New York: Doubleday & Company, 1941.
    One of the first archaeological histories of the Aztec, and still the most complete. It was written by the best-grounded of all the present-day scholars and although written for the general reader, it suggests the method of Vaillant's thinking. His suicide with a revolver at the edge of his swimming pool, into which his body fell, in 1945, to make death doubly certain, on the eve of being sent on a mission to Spain, still remains unexplained and inexplicable.

42. *Ibid.*

43. Victor W. von Hagen, *Realm of the Incas,* New York: The New American Library (Mentor Books), 1957.

44. Oswald Spengler, *op. cit.*

45. John H. Cornyn (ed. and tr.), "Aztec Literature," in *The Song of Quetzalcoatl,* Yellow Spring, Ohio: The Antioch Press, 1931.
    Bernal Díaz del Castillo, *op. cit.*

46. John Alden Mason, "Native Languages of Middle America," in *The Maya and Their Neighbors,* by George C. Vaillant and others, New York: D. Appleton-Century Co., 1941, pp. 52–87.

47. John H. Cornyn, *op. cit.*

48. Miguel León Portilla, *La Filosofía Nahuatl,* Mexico, 1956.
    An unusually profound and thoroughly documented work using the remains of the Aztec literature to suggest the complex Aztec interest in the world about him. The selection of the material, its elucidation through actual Aztec texts, provides another aspect of Aztec life, otherwise missing in the literature about them.

49. Tacitus, *Germania,* tr. by H. Mattingly, Harmondsworth, England: Penguin Books, Ltd., 1948.

50. V. Gordon Childe, "Early Forms of Society," in *A History of Technology,* ed. by Charles J. Singer and others, New

York and London: Oxford University Press, 1954, pp. 38–57. A magnificent and encyclopedic volume (827 pp.) to provide students of technology, science and archaeologists with some human and historical background for studies of pre-literate societies. A pioneer work, each part written by a specialist in its field, it deals mostly with the Near East and the civilizations about the fertile crescent. It seldom enters the "American theater" and when it does it is usually wrong, e.g., the Chimu culture of Peru is dated 1200 B.C. (actually A.D. 1000) on p. 731; its information on Peru's roads is hopelessly entangled.

51. George C. Vaillant, *op. cit.*

52. Antonius Mendoza, *Codice Mendocino*, 2 vols., Mexico, 1925.

53. Aldous Huxley, *Beyond the Mexique Bay*, London: Chatto & Windus; New York: Harper & Brothers, 1934.
A charmingly small book on the effect of Middle America and Mexico on Aldous Huxley. All of the conclusions are Huxleian, always stimulating and with a slant which the professional scholar has not seen or does not see.

54. George C. Vaillant, *op. cit.*

55. Antonius Mendoza, *op. cit.*

56. Jacques Soustelle, *op. cit.*

57. George C. Vaillant, *op. cit.*

58. Benvenuto Cellini, *Autobiography*, tr. by J. A. Symonds, New York: Garden City Publishing Co., 1937.

59. R. H. Barrow, *The Romans*, Harmondsworth, England: Penguin Books, Ltd., 1949.

60. F. E. Zeuner, "Cultivation of Plants," in *A History of Technology, op. cit.*, p. 353 f.

61. Carl O. Sauer, "Cultivated Plants of South and Central America," in *Handbook of South American Indians*, vol. 6, Washington, 1950, pp. 487–543.

62. *Ibid.*

63. S. G. Morley, *The Ancient Maya*, Palo Alto: Stanford University Press, 1946; London: Oxford University Press, 1947.

64. Woodrow Borah, *Early Colonial Trade and Navigation between Mexico and Peru,* Berkeley: University of California Press (Ibero-Americana, 38), 1954.

65. Thor Heyerdahl, *Kon-Tiki: Across the Pacific by Raft,* tr. by F. H. Lyon, Chicago: Rand-McNally; London: George Allen & Unwin, Ltd., 1950.

66. José de Acosta, *History of the East and West Indies,* London, 1604.
    A very learned and balanced Jesuit, whose intellectual love of God did not blind him to the good qualities of the Indian; this book is notable since it deals with Acosta's travels in Mexico and Peru as early as 1595. He compares the cultures, he is colorful and accurate. When obtained (which will be difficult) the work should be read.

67. George C. Vaillant, *op. cit.*

68. J. A. Brillat-Savarin, *Physiologie du Goût,* tr. by Arthur Machen, London, 1925.

69. Bernardino de Sahagun, *Historia General de las Cosas de Nueva España,* 3 vols., Mexico, 1952.

70. Aldous Huxley, *op. cit.*

71. Bernal Díaz del Castillo, *op. cit.*

72. Hernando Cortés, *op. cit.*

73. Bernal Díaz del Castillo, *op. cit.*

74. Lucien Lévy-Bruhl, *Primitives and the Supernatural,* tr. by Lilian A. Clare, New York: E. P. Dutton & Co., Inc., 1935; London: George Allen & Unwin, Ltd., 1936.
    Considerable insight into the idea of confession as it has come up from the outer spaces of primitivity is given by Lucien Lévy-Bruhl and with it an understanding of the metaphysics (dialectics in the Soviet unreason) of confession. Among primitives, as long as the doer of a deed keeps it a secret, it is like a being that has issued from itself living a life of its own, engendering fatal consequences. The essential reason for the confession is that it is tantamount to a disenchantment. A person who stubbornly refuses to confess is therefore a public enemy. Torture has everywhere been the companion of confession . . . whether it is Fiji, Eskimo, Bantu or Russian; one must confess at all costs. There are no scruples effected in this, for the enormity of

the charge does away with any need to seek for proofs; besides, the trial by ordeal is infallible and nobody would dream of wanting any confirmation of it. See page 356.

75. Anatole France, *At the Sign of the Reine Pédauque*, London, 1923.

76. Victor von Klarwill (ed.), *The Fugger News-Letters*, tr. by Pauline de Chary, New York: G. P. Putnam's Sons, 1925. (First Series).

77. William Gates (ed.), *The de la Cruz-Badiano Aztec Herbal of 1552*, New York: The Maya Society, 1939.

78. Jacques Soustelle, *op. cit.*

79. Anonymous Conqueror, *op. cit.*

80. George C. Vaillant, *op. cit.*

81. *Ibid.*

82. V. Gordon Childe, *op. cit.*

83. Henry R. Wagner, *The Rise of Fernando Cortés*, Berkeley: University of California Press (Cortés Society, Bancroft Library), 1944.

84. Jacques Soustelle, *op. cit.*

85. George C. Vaillant, *op. cit.*

86. Ignacio Marquina, *op. cit.*
Tenayuca Official Guide, Mexico, n.d.

87. Ignacio Marquina, "Calixtlahuaca," in *op. cit.*, pp. 223-38.

88. ———, "Malinalco," in *op. cit.*, pp. 204–16.
José García Payón, "Malinalco," *Revista Mexicana de Estudios Antropológicos*, tomo viii, Mexico, 1946.

89. George C. Vaillant, *op. cit.*

90. V. Gordon Childe, *op. cit.*

91. Ignacio Marquina, "Tula," in *op. cit.*, pp. 145–64.

92. Bernal Díaz del Castillo, *op. cit.*
Hernando Cortés, *op. cit.*

93. Bernal Díaz del Castillo, *op. cit.*

94. S. G. Morley, *op. cit.*

95. George C. Vaillant, *op. cit.*

96. Ignacio Marquina, "Cempoala," in *op. cit.*, pp. 460–79.

97. Alfonso Caso, *Las Exploraciones en Monte Albán, 1934–35,* Mexico: Instituto Panamericano de Geografía é Historia, No. 19, 1935.
    One of the great figures in Mexican archaeology. His explorations into and the restoration of Monte Albán, an Olmec-Zapotec-Mixtec religious site in Oaxaca, gave us more than 1500 years of chronology. His discovery of the famous golden jewels at Monte Albán in an untouched, unrifled tomb gave the physical evidence of the excellence of Mexican goldsmithery.
    Lorenzo Gamio, *Archaeological Guide of Monte Albán,* Mexico, n.d.
    Ignacio Marquina, "Monte Albán," in *op. cit.*, pp. 311–61.

98. Aldous Huxley, *op. cit.*

99. Pál Kelemen, *Medieval American Art,* 2 vols., New York: The Macmillan Company, 1943.
    This, the mature work of a Hungarian-born and -educated art historian, has a freshness and directness not always found in literature on the Maya and Aztec. He treats the objects as art, not as potsherds; his observations, since they are neither hipped nor dulled by the standard archaeological vocabulary, are thought-evoking. It should be read by any who wish to push their interest in American cultures beyond the dim outline of general books.

100. Salvador de Madariaga, *Hernán Cortés, Conqueror of Mexico,* New York: The Macmillan Company, 1941; London: Hodder & Stoughton, Ltd., 1942.

101. Hernando Cortés, *op. cit.*

102. Miguel León Portilla, *op. cit.*

103. A. M. Garibay, *Historia de la Literatura Nahuatl,* 2 vols., Mexico, 1953–54.

104. Maurice Collis, *op. cit.*

105. Alfonso Caso, *El Pueblo del Sol,* Mexico, 1953.

106. Franz Boas (ed.), *General Anthropology*, Boston: D. C. Heath, 1938; London: George G. Harrap, 1939.

107. O. Neugebauer, "Ancient Mathematics and Astronomy," in *A History of Technology, op. cit.,* pp. 785–803.

108. *Ibid.*

109. Oswald Spengler, *op. cit.*

110. George C. Vaillant, *op. cit.*

111. Marshall Saville, *Tizoc, Great Lord of the Aztec,* New York: Museum of the American Indian-Heye Foundation, 1929.

112. V. Gordon Childe, *op. cit.*

113. Samuel K. Lothrop, "South America as Seen from Middle America," in *The Maya and Their Neighbors, op. cit.,* pp. 417–29.

114. Victor W. von Hagen, *Highway of the Sun,* New York: Duell, Sloan & Pearce, 1955.

115. Alfonso Villa, "The Yaxuna-Coba Causeway," in *American Archaeology,* Vol. 11, No. 9, Washington, Institute of Washington, Pub. No. 436, 1934.

116. Woodrow, Borah, *op. cit.*

117. Dard Hunter, *Papermaking: The History and Technique of an Ancient Craft* (2nd ed. rev. & enl.), New York: Alfred A. Knopf, 1947; London: Pleiades Books, Ltd., 1948.

118. Victor W. von Hagen, *The Aztec and Maya Papermakers,* New York: J. J. Augustin, 1943.
———, *La Fabricación del Papel entre los Aztecas y los Mayas,* Mexico, 1945.
———, "Mexican Papermaking Plants," *Journal of the New York Botanical Gardens,* Vol. 44, New York, 1943.
———, *The Jicaque Indians of Honduras,* New York: Museum of the American Indian-Heye Foundation, 1943.
———, "Paper and Civilization," *Scientific Monthly,* Vol. LVII, Washington, 1943, pp. 301–14.
———, *Francisco Hernández, op. cit.*

120. Dard Hunter, *Chinese Ceremonial Paper,* Chillicothe, Ohio, 1937.

121. H. S. Hooke, "Recording and Writing," in *A History of Technology, op. cit.*, pp. 774 *et. seq.*

122. *Ibid.*

123. Pál Kelemen, *op. cit.*

124. A. M. Garibay, *op. cit.*

125. Robert Graves, *The White Goddess,* New York: Creative Age Press, 1948; London: Faber & Faber, Ltd.

126. A. M. Garibay, *op. cit.*

127. Miguel León Portilla, *op. cit.*

128. *Ibid.*

129. Waldo Frank, *America Hispaña: A Portrait and a Prospect,* New York: Charles Scribner's Sons, 1931.

INDEX

The MENTOR Religious Classics

The Holy Bible in Brief *edited and arranged by James Reeves.* The basic story of the Old and New Testaments, a continuous narrative in the words of the King James text.
(#Ms116—50¢)

The Meaning of the Glorious Koran: An Explanatory Translation *by Mohammed Marmaduke Pickthall.* The complete sacred book of Mohammedanism. (#MT223—75¢)

The Teachings of the Compassionate Buddha *edited with commentary by E. A. Burtt.* The best translations of the writings of the great Oriental religion of Buddhism.
(#MD131—50¢)

The Song of God: Bhagavad-Gita *translated by Swami Prabhavananda and Christopher Isherwood.* The timeless epic of Hindu faith. Introduction *by Aldous Huxley.*
(#MD103—50¢)

The Upanishads: Breath of the Eternal *translated by Swami Prabhavananda and Frederick Manchester.* Concerned with the knowledge of God and the highest aspects of religious truth, these ancient Hindu scriptures are presented in a readable translation. (#MD194—50¢)

The Way of Life: Tao Te Ching, *by Lao Tzu.* A masterpiece of ancient Chinese wisdom, translated by *R. B. Blakney,* presenting the philosophy of Taoism. (#MD129—50¢)

The Sayings of Confucius: A New Translation *by James R. Ware.* The sayings of the greatest wise man of ancient China, teaching the ageless virtues of civilized men.
(#MD151—50¢)

The Living Talmud: The Wisdom of the Fathers and Its Classical Commentaries, *selected and translated by Judah Goldin.* A new translation, with an illuminating essay on the place of the Talmud in Jewish life and religion.
(#MD199—50¢)

The Authentic New Testament *translated by Hugh J. Schonfield.* A new translation by a Jewish scholar conveying the authentic atmosphere and style of the original New Testament documents. (#MD215—50¢)

Other MENTOR Books of Special Interest

Patterns of Culture *by Ruth Benedict.* A famous anthropologist analyzes our social structure in relation to primitive cultures.   (#MD89—50¢)

Human Types *by Raymond Firth.* An introduction to social anthropology, analyzing the types of mankind, their origin, differences, and similarities.   (#MD227—50¢)

Man: His First Million Years *by Ashley Montagu.* A vivid, lively account of the origin of man and the development of his races, cultures, customs, and beliefs. (#MD239—50¢)

The Origin of Species *by Charles Darwin.* Introduction *by Sir Julian Huxley.* The classic work on man's evolution, that revolutionized scientific and religious thinking from the 19th century onwards.   (#MD222—50¢)

Evolution in Action *by Julian Huxley.* A world-famous biologist describes the process of evolution and shows that man now has the power to shape his future development.
(#MD204—50¢)

Male and Female *by Margaret Mead.* Explores the sexual patterns of modern men and women and discusses childhood, courtship, love and marriage in the South Seas and America.
(#MD150—50¢)

The Meaning of Evolution (revised, abridged) *by George Gaylord Simpson.* Outlines the whole course of life on earth and its ethical implications for mankind. (#MD66—50¢)
